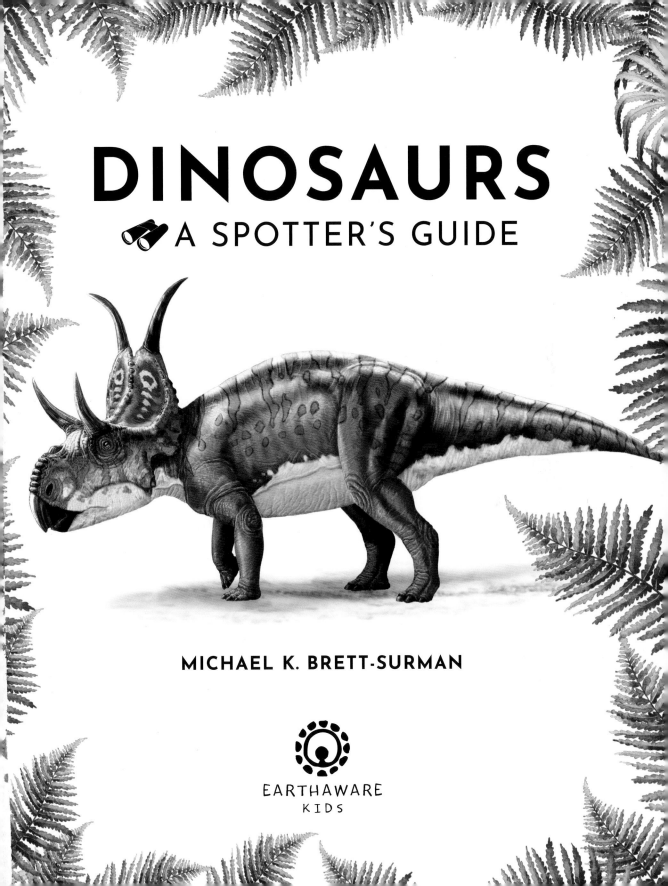

DINOSAURS
A SPOTTER'S GUIDE

MICHAEL K. BRETT-SURMAN

EARTHAWARE
KIDS

Written by: Michael K. Brett-Surman
Consultant: Dr. Neil Clark, Hunterian Museum

Illustrated by: Anne Bowman, John Bull, Peter Bull Art Studio, Leonello Calvetti, Barry Croucher/The Art Agency, Wendy de Paauw, Simone End, Christer Eriksson, Cecilia Fitzsimons/The Art Agency, Chris Forsey, John Francis/Bernard Thornton Artists UK, Murray Frederick, Lee Gibbons, Malcolm Godwin, Gino Hasler, Philip Hood/The Art Agency, Robert Haynes, Steve Kirk/The Art Agency, David Kirshner, Frank Knight, David McAllister, James McKinnon, James McKinnon and Peter Bull Art Studio, Colin Newman/Bernard Thornton Artists UK, Nicola Oram, Pixelshack, Mick Posen/The Art Agency, Tony Pyrzakowski, Luis Rey/The Art Agency, John Richards, Andrew Robinson/Garden Studio, Peter Schouten, Peter Scott/The Art Agency, Marco Sparaciari, Kevin Stead, Franco Tempeta, Anne Winterbotham

EARTHAWARE
KIDS

Published by EarthAware Kids

Created by Weldon Owen Children's Books
A subsidiary of Insight International, L.P.
PO Box 3088
San Rafael, CA 94912
www.insighteditions.com

Weldon Owen Children's Books
Designer: Karen Wilks
Editor: George Maudsley
Assistant Editor: Pandita Geary

Art Director: Stuart Smith
Senior Production Manager: Greg Steffen
Publisher: Sue Grabham

Insight Editions
Publisher: Raoul Goff

ISBN: 978-1-68188-793-7
Manufactured, printed and assembled in China
First printing, July 2021 TOM/07/21
25 24 23 22 2 3 4 5 6 7 8

Futalognkosaurus

Stegosaurus

Fruitadens

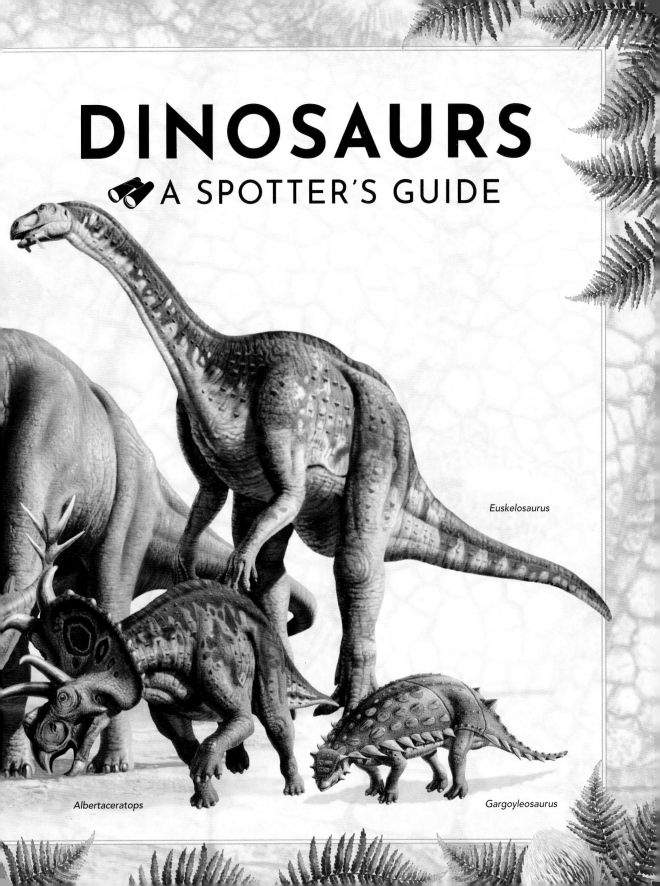

DINOSAURS
A SPOTTER'S GUIDE

Euskelosaurus

Albertaceratops

Gargoyleosaurus

CONTENTS

INTRODUCING DINOSAURS

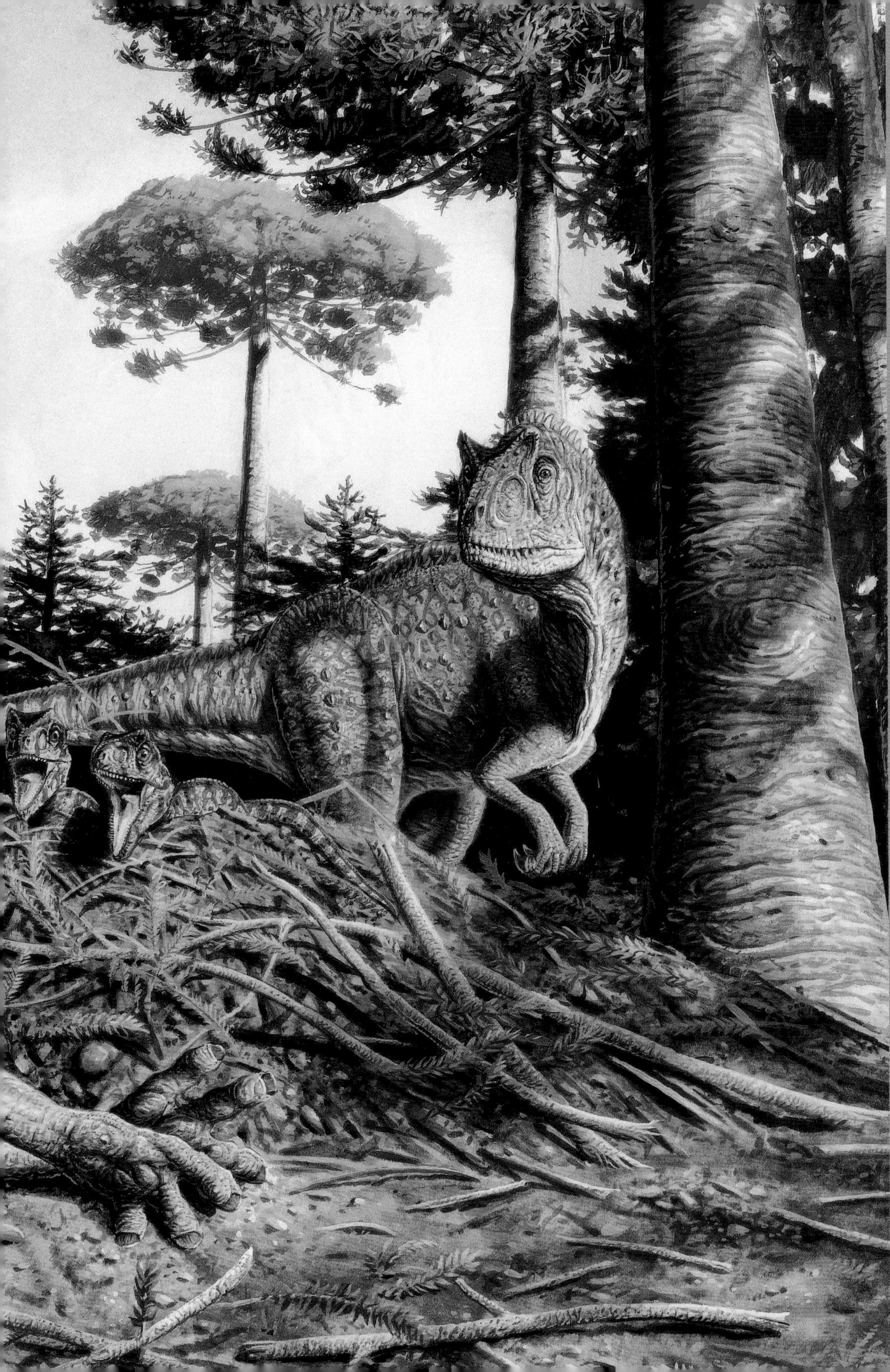

WHAT IS A DINOSAUR?

We have discovered the fossils of more than 1,000 different kinds of dinosaur. The word dinosaur means "terrible lizard," but this does not apply to all dinosaurs. Some were bigger than a bus, but others were as small as a chicken. Dinosaurs of all sizes had lots of things in common. They all walked with their legs directly under their bodies, and they are the only reptiles ever to do this. They laid eggs, and while some had scaly skin, many also had featherlike coverings.

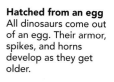

Hatched from an egg
All dinosaurs come out of an egg. Their armor, spikes, and horns develop as they get older.

Fused bones
The hip bone is fused to the backbone for extra strength. Together, these bones are called the sacrum.

Allosaurus

Stegosaurus

Camptosaurus

Tyrannosaurus

Saltasaurus

Coelurus

Euoplocephalus   Pachycephalosaurus   Corythosaurus

Triceratops

Hip bones
The hip bone supports the muscles that grip the thighbone tightly. Other muscles move the legs backward and forward.

COMMON ANCESTORS

Dinosaurs come in many different sizes, shapes, and colors. They come with and without armor, horns, beaks, and claws, but they are all classified as belonging to the same group as one or other of the first two dinosaurs to be scientifically named —*Iguanodon* and *Megalosaurus*. *Asilisaurus*, a possible common ancestor to all dinosaurs, was found in Tanzania in 2010.

Head
Some dinosaurs have strange headgear. This crest is used either to attract a mate or to ward off rivals.

Upright stance
Legs directly under the body allow the limbs to support very heavy bodies. They also allow for a longer stride.

Longest finger
The longest finger of the hand, especially in theropods, is designed to grasp.

DILOPHOSAURUS
This Triassic theropod is typical of early two-legged dinosaurs. The arms no longer support weight, as with four-legged dinosaurs, but are adapted for hunting. The center of mass has moved back toward the pelvis, which makes balancing on two legs easier.

WHAT IS NOT A DINOSAUR?
During the Mesozoic era (252–66 mya), there were up to 40 groups of reptiles, but only two of these included dinosaurs. Dinosaurs did not live in the sea, but some of their distant relatives ruled the ancient oceans. With the exception of pterosaurs, almost all the other groups had a sprawling stance. Early dinosaurs could not fly —pterosaurs, or flying reptiles, did that.

Pterosaurs
Pterosaurs were cousins of dinosaurs. There were two groups: rhamphorhynchoids (dominant in the Jurassic) and pterodactyls (dominant in the Cretaceous).

Scaphognathus

Nothosaurs
Ocean-dwelling reptiles, whose name means "false lizard." They were similar to the later plesiosaurs but thrived during the Triassic.

Nothosaurus

Pelycosaurs
These synapsids, once called "mammal-like reptiles," were reptilelike tetrapods that evolved into mammals. *Dimetrodon* lived 75 million years before the dinosaurs.

Dimetrodon

Pliosaurs
This group of marine predators had a short neck and an elongated head, unlike their relatives, the long-necked plesiosaurs.

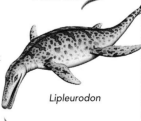

Lipleurodon

Crocodiles
There used to be dozens of species of crocodile. Some lived on land and others in the sea. *Bernissartia* was the smallest, at only 2 feet long.

Bernissartia

DINOSAUR WEIGH-IN

The dinosaurs include some of the largest and longest animals ever to have lived. During their 165 million years on Earth, different groups of dinosaurs adapted to many surroundings. They lived in most regions and most climates. They also had to adapt to other animals, including other dinosaurs that competed with them for food and shelter. There were two-legged meat-eaters; long-necked, four-legged plant-eaters; two-legged plant-eaters; two-legged plant-eaters with duck-bills; four-legged, horned plant-eaters with short tails; and many more!

DUCK-BILLED DINOSAURS

Duck-billed dinosaurs use their beaks to cut off leaves and stalks to eat. They have hundreds of cheek teeth for chewing food before swallowing it. Each of the four jawbones has three rows of 60 teeth—a total of 720 teeth.

A duck-billed dinosaur's wide "bill" is an expanded nasal bone covered in skin, or a horny beak.

Lambeosaurus
This duck-billed dinosaur makes hornlike sounds using a hollow crest on top of its head.

NO WAY!
There is no such thing as a typical dinosaur. There are too many different types of dinosaurs to work out an "average" size, length or weight.

STEGOSAUR

Stegosaurus has a small head compared to the rest of its body. It is a four-legged, armored plant-eater.

CERATOPSIAN

Albertaceratops has horns and spikes on its head but not on its body. It is a four-legged plant-eater with a short tail.

LONG-NECKED SAUROPOD
Patagotitan is a long-necked, four-legged plant-eater. It is one of the largest animals ever to have lived, growing to about 120 feet long and weighing more than 66 tons.

THEROPODS
Most theropods are two-legged meat-eaters. Most are lightly built with large heads. They usually have bladelike, serrated teeth (teeth with sawlike edges) that they use to tear up their food before they swallow it.

Dilong
Theropods are the first animals to stand on two legs and the first to have feathers. *Dilong* has body feathers but cannot fly.

Eocarcharia
This fierce-looking theropod uses its sawlike teeth to rip apart its prey. Its name means "dawn shark."

PACHYCEPHALOSAUR
This young pachycephalosaur has horns and bumps on its head. It is a two-legged plant-eater. Pachycephalosaur means "thick-headed lizard."

ANKYLOSAUR
Struthiosaurus is one of the smallest ankylosaurs, or four-legged, armored plant-eaters. It is only 7 feet long.

DIFFERENT HIP BONES

Dinosaurs are divided into two major groups: the saurischian ("lizard-hipped") dinosaurs and the ornithischian ("bird-hipped") dinosaurs. The hip, or the pelvis, is made up of three bones—the pubis, ilium, and ischium. Muscles connected the pubis to the ribs, which helped saurischians to breathe and supported the gut. The pubis pointed forward and downward in saurischians, and backward in the plant-eating ornithischians. In ornithischians, the pubis acted more as an aid to breathing than as support for the gut.

NO WAY!

Even though ornithischians are "bird-hipped," birds evolved from the saurischians.

Ischium
Points backward. It supports muscles that hold the tail off the ground.

Ilium
Supports the leg muscles. It transfers leg movement to the rest of the body.

Pubis
Points forward in saurischians. It helps to support strong gut muscles.

ALLOSAURUS
This saurischian dinosaur is a meat-eater that lives in the Late Jurassic.

SAURISCHIAN DINOSAURS
Note the hole in the middle of the pelvis of this *Allosaurus*. This is where the thighbone of both saurischians and ornithischians is inserted. The "rocker" at the end of the pubis takes the weight of this predatory theropod when it lowers itself to the ground to rest.

STANDING UPRIGHT

The hip bones of all dinosaurs are connected to the leg bones in the same way. They stand upright, and can walk farther and faster than sprawling reptiles, whose legs point outward.

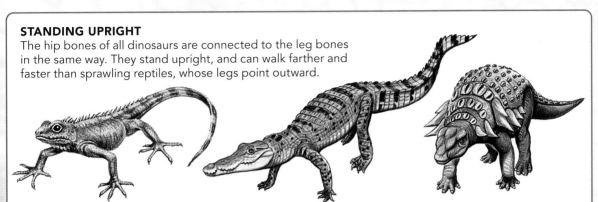

Legs out
Lizards' legs are sprawled. They swing them out to move. This limits how much weight they can carry.

Under or out
Crocodiles are semisprawled. They can carry heavier weights but cannot run far on land.

Legs under
Dinosaurs can swing their limbs forward and backward underneath them—an efficient way of moving.

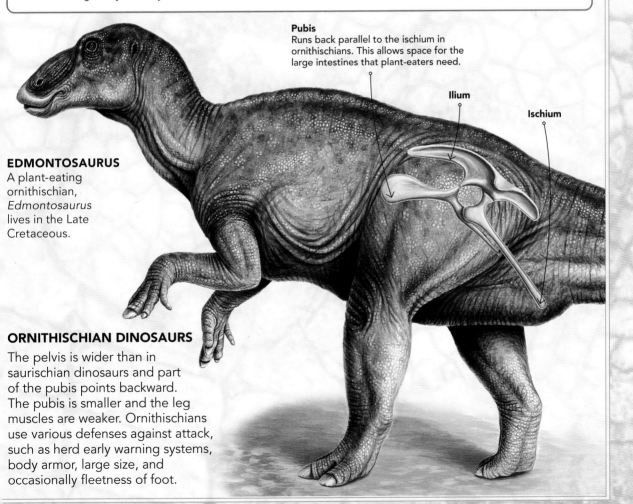

Pubis
Runs back parallel to the ischium in ornithischians. This allows space for the large intestines that plant-eaters need.

Ilium

Ischium

EDMONTOSAURUS

A plant-eating ornithischian, *Edmontosaurus* lives in the Late Cretaceous.

ORNITHISCHIAN DINOSAURS

The pelvis is wider than in saurischian dinosaurs and part of the pubis points backward. The pubis is smaller and the leg muscles are weaker. Ornithischians use various defenses against attack, such as herd early warning systems, body armor, large size, and occasionally fleetness of foot.

FEEDING

Plant-eating dinosaurs ate the plants that were most abundant at the time—cycads, ferns, and conifers. These are much less nutritious than today's flowering plants, so plant-eating dinosaurs had to eat all the time. Their food passed into their huge guts and stayed there for a long time to squeeze every bit of nutrition out of it. Meat-eating dinosaurs had fearsome weapons, including foot claws, hand claws, and teeth. Other dinosaurs defended themselves from these weapons with body armor or spikes, or simply by running away!

STEGOSAURUS

This armored plant-eater feeds on cycads, conifers, and ferns. These plants only grow back slowly, so *Stegosaurus* was constantly on the move in search of new plants to eat.

TEETH AND JAWS

The earliest plant-eating dinosaurs have thick teeth covered with enamel. Later dinosaurs have enamel only on one side. As the teeth from their upper and lower jaws grind up the plant matter, the softer side wears away faster than the enamel. This makes the teeth self-sharpening. They are also constantly replaced. We only get two sets of teeth in our entire lifetime, but dinosaurs get all they need!

Othnielia eats small leaves. Some of its teeth are only 1/8 inch above the gum line so they eat the softest leaves they can find.

NO WAY!

Some dinosaurs swallow stones. Their gizzard (a muscular organ) crashes the stones together to grind up their food.

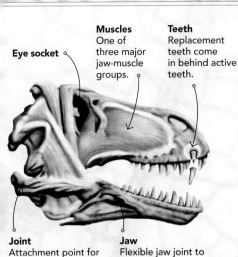

Eye socket

Muscles
One of three major jaw-muscle groups.

Teeth
Replacement teeth come in behind active teeth.

Joint
Attachment point for massive neck.

Jaw
Flexible jaw joint to prevent dislocation.

BONE CRUNCHER

Tyrannosaurus has powerful jaw muscles that help it to crunch up the bones of its prey. The heavy jaw has an extra joint in the middle, which allows the mouth to open wide and take extra-large bites. Bony bits protect the eyes from being damaged by struggling prey.

QUICK ESCAPE

Triassic meat-eaters chase a lizard that is about to escape up a tree. Triassic theropods have not yet achieved their giant sizes, so any prey that can get 10 feet off the ground is safe—unless a flying pterosaur is nearby.

Fern

NO WAY!

Tyrant is the name given to a harsh ruler. The name *Tyrannosaurus* means "tyrant lizard."

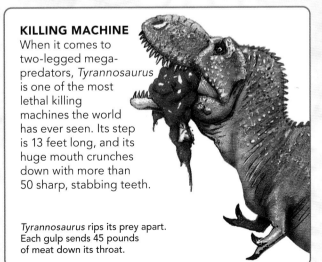

KILLING MACHINE

When it comes to two-legged mega-predators, *Tyrannosaurus* is one of the most lethal killing machines the world has ever seen. Its step is 13 feet long, and its huge mouth crunches down with more than 50 sharp, stabbing teeth.

Tyrannosaurus rips its prey apart. Each gulp sends 45 pounds of meat down its throat.

ANATOMY OF A DINOSAUR

A dinosaur's body was similar to those of many of today's land animals, but it was closest in structure to crocodiles and birds. Two-legged dinosaurs sometimes had arms for grabbing, and sometimes their arms were for flying or gliding. All dinosaurs' necks had to be flexible enough to reach food, and their heads had to be big enough to eat the food. Their bodies also had to be large enough to process the food and breathe. Dinosaurs' legs had to be strong enough to hold their bodies off the ground so that they could walk or run. Their tails had to be long and heavy enough to provide balance or act as a weapon.

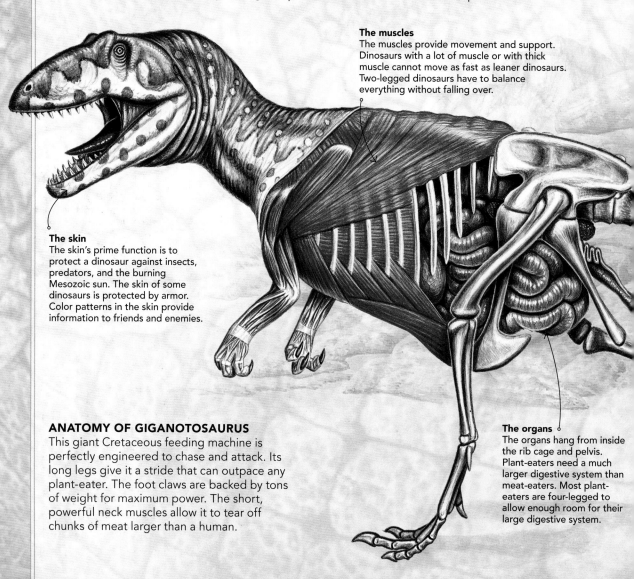

The muscles
The muscles provide movement and support. Dinosaurs with a lot of muscle or with thick muscle cannot move as fast as leaner dinosaurs. Two-legged dinosaurs have to balance everything without falling over.

The skin
The skin's prime function is to protect a dinosaur against insects, predators, and the burning Mesozoic sun. The skin of some dinosaurs is protected by armor. Color patterns in the skin provide information to friends and enemies.

ANATOMY OF GIGANOTOSAURUS
This giant Cretaceous feeding machine is perfectly engineered to chase and attack. Its long legs give it a stride that can outpace any plant-eater. The foot claws are backed by tons of weight for maximum power. The short, powerful neck muscles allow it to tear off chunks of meat larger than a human.

The organs
The organs hang from inside the rib cage and pelvis. Plant-eaters need a much larger digestive system than meat-eaters. Most plant-eaters are four-legged to allow enough room for their large digestive system.

ORGANS AND MUSCLES

Every once in a great while, palaeontologists get lucky and dinosaur fossils preserve internal organs, muscles, and skin. By looking inside the stone that surrounds the fossils using the latest technology, palaeontologists do not have to spend years carefully taking away rock. The scan of one small fossil of meat-eater *Scipionyx* shows the outline of its liver!

Soft tissue

The information about the organs of this *Brachylophosaurus* was taken from a fossil that had fossilized soft tissue around its skeleton. This gave many clues to the dinosaur's anatomy.

NO WAY!

Scientists learn how dinosaurs walk by studying ostriches, which have a very similar leg anatomy.

The bones

Bones have roles other than weight-bearing. Bones of the neck and legs are hollow in many two-legged meat-eaters. This allows them to move faster. Some bones are unique to certain dinosaurs, so palaeontologists can often identify a species from a single bone fragment.

Sail

The many blood vessels in the skin make it easy to quickly heat up or cool down the body of *Ouranosaurus*. The entire sail is anchored to the backbone.

OURANOSAURUS SAIL

The sail on *Ouranosaurus* is 3 feet tall. It is used to regulate temperature, to display threat, and for recognition. It also makes *Ouranosaurus* look much bigger than it actually is, which is important when hungry theropods are around.

Protection

Adults may use their own bodies to shade newly hatched babies that have not yet grown sails of their own.

SKELETONS, SKULLS, AND SKIN

Two-legged dinosaurs used their arms for defense or to gather food, and often ran at high speeds on their two legs. Four-legged dinosaurs were generally much heavier and slower. Dinosaur skin had to be thick enough to protect against insects and scrapes. It may have changed color in some small dinosaurs for extra camouflage.

Skull
Eyes face forward, which limits range of vision but also improves accuracy.

Tail
The long tail is a counterbalance to the front of the dinosaur.

Hips
The hips are wide to make room for a plant-eater's guts.

Backbone
Hardened tissue between the bones makes the backbone rigid.

Leg bones
The legs are long and lightly built for speed and agility.

Hands
Hands grasp plants and pull down branches.

Feet
Long toes similar to a bird's make this dinosaur flexible.

HYPSILOPHODON

This small plant-eater is quite common in the Early Cretaceous. It feeds on soft plants that are less than 6 feet high, and may also eat small animals.

DINOSAUR SKULLS

In the skulls of plant-eaters, the joint between the upper and lower jaw lies below the level of the teeth. This makes the jaws come together like a nutcracker. The skulls of meat-eaters have the jaw joint in line with the teeth, so their jaws come together like a pair of scissors.

Ouranosaurus is a plant-eater with many teeth located back toward its jaw joint. This gives the jaws a powerful grinding action.

Ceratosaurus is a meat-eater with teeth at the front of its mouth. The jaw muscles put the main force of the bite at the front.

Tail
Tails can contain more than 50 bones. They are carried off the ground.

Hips
The hips are fused to five bones in the spine for added strength.

Hind feet
Thick pads on the feet absorb the weight.

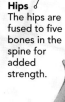

Bone strength
Near the backbone, dinosaur skin contains large, bony plates. They make the skin very tough.

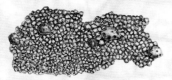

Flexible skin
Closer to the belly, the scales and bony plates are smaller, which makes the skin more flexible. This allows the belly to bulge with food.

Feathers
Feathers may cover the skin of the earliest dinosaurs, although there are not enough fossils for us to be sure. Many later dinosaurs have a scaly covering.

COLORS AND MARKINGS
It can be difficult to work out what colors dinosaurs are, but some fossils give us a good idea. *Anchiornis'* fossilized feathers tell us it is black with white wing tips, and has a red crown. Other dinosaurs may be striped, spotted ,or brightly colored.

CREATIVE COLOR
Some scientists believe that dinosaurs are dull to hide from predators or prey. Others think that some, such as the duck-billed dinosaurs, change color to mate or to defend their territories.

Skull
The hollow areas are actually filled with jaw muscles.

Backbone
Each bone has extra tissue connections—one in front and one behind.

Stripes
Stripes are a form of camouflage and help to break up an animal's outline.

Spots
Spots are another way to blend into the background.

CAMARASAURUS
This giant sauropod from the Late Jurassic is the most common plant-eater in the Morrison Formation in the USA. It feeds on fibrous plants up to 20 feet off the ground. It has the strongest teeth of any Jurassic dinosaur.

Dull
Dull colors are sometimes the best defense. Large plant-eaters usually blend in with their environment's shades of browns and grays.

Chest
The chest is barrel-shaped to "hang" the guts off the ribs.

Front legs
Pillarlike thick limbs support the animal's weight.

Front feet
One giant claw is all the defense it needs.

BRAINS AND COMMUNICATION

All animals with a backbone have brains, with parts for thinking, feeling, moving, and sensing. Scientists work out the size and shape of dinosaur brains from the space they leave within the fossil skull. All dinosaurs had tiny brains compared to humans. The brain of a small meat-eater was relatively larger than the brain of a huge plant-eater, because a meat-eater had to be smart enough to hunt.

BRAIN

If you compare a mammal and a dinosaur of the same size, the brain of the mammal is much larger. Mammals are much smarter than dinosaurs, but some dinosaurs have brains that are almost as big as the brains of some modern-day birds.

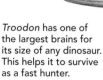

Stegosaurus has the smallest brain of any ornithischian, but its tiny brain serves it well for millions of years.

Troodon has one of the largest brains for its size of any dinosaur. This helps it to survive as a fast hunter.

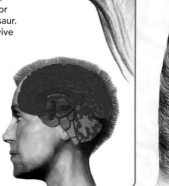

Humans have the largest brain of all terrestrial (land-based) animals. A human brain occupies most of the head.

SMELL AND TASTE

Dinosaurs can taste the air with specialized cells in the mouth. This helps them to find food and avoid predators.

Iguanodon has a good sense of smell and taste. It may be able to smell hidden predators.

SIGHT

Most plant-eaters have eyes that face in different directions, which gives them a wide field of vision. Many meat-eaters have eyes that face forward, which gives them a limited field of vision but increased accuracy and depth perception.

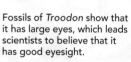

Fossils of *Troodon* show that it has large eyes, which leads scientists to believe that it has good eyesight.

HEARING

Dinosaurs have one large ear bone and can hear low-frequency sounds. Mammals have three small ear bones and can hear high-frequency sounds. It is possible that dinosaurs can hear frequencies too low for humans, as crocodiles can.

Saurolophus makes honking sounds, so its hearing is probably good enough to hear responses from others.

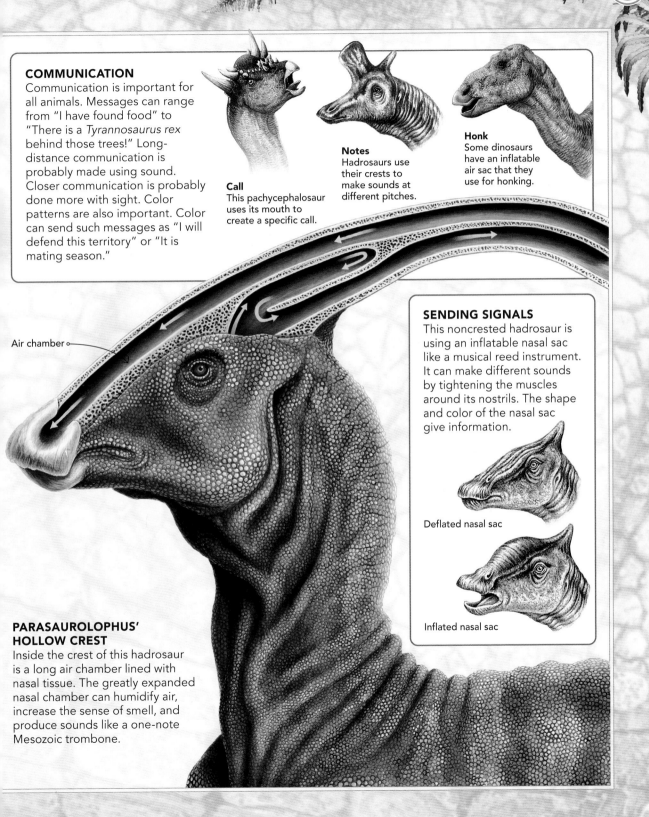

COMMUNICATION

Communication is important for all animals. Messages can range from "I have found food" to "There is a *Tyrannosaurus rex* behind those trees!" Long-distance communication is probably made using sound. Closer communication is probably done more with sight. Color patterns are also important. Color can send such messages as "I will defend this territory" or "It is mating season."

Call
This pachycephalosaur uses its mouth to create a specific call.

Notes
Hadrosaurs use their crests to make sounds at different pitches.

Honk
Some dinosaurs have an inflatable air sac that they use for honking.

Air chamber

SENDING SIGNALS

This noncrested hadrosaur is using an inflatable nasal sac like a musical reed instrument. It can make different sounds by tightening the muscles around its nostrils. The shape and color of the nasal sac give information.

Deflated nasal sac

Inflated nasal sac

PARASAUROLOPHUS' HOLLOW CREST

Inside the crest of this hadrosaur is a long air chamber lined with nasal tissue. The greatly expanded nasal chamber can humidify air, increase the sense of smell, and produce sounds like a one-note Mesozoic trombone.

EGGS AND BABIES

Dinosaurs had a variety of nesting behaviors. Some nests were isolated, while others were laid in groups close to each other. Some dinosaurs did not make nests at all but laid their eggs on the ground. Some adult dinosaurs cared for their young, as birds do. Others abandoned their eggs in the way that many lizards and turtles do today.

Independent
When a meat-eating theropod hatches from its egg, it will be cared for by its mother for just a short time before going its own way.

Dependent
Born with weak bones, plant-eaters are looked after until they are strong enough to leave.

EGG-LAYING PATTERN

Dinosaurs lay their eggs in many different ways. Some make nests, line them to keep the eggs warm, and lay their eggs in a particular pattern. Others seem to lay them on the ground in no pattern at all. Some dinosaurs have colored or speckled eggs.

Plant-eating sauropods lay their eggs in an arc shape across the ground.

Hadrosaurs lay their eggs in a spiral pattern in a shallow, lined nest.

Some small meat-eaters lay their eggs side by side to form two rows in the nest.

No one knows which dinosaur made this nest. The eggs are scattered.

Maiasaura nests contain up to 25 eggs. The nest is scooped out of mud in the shape of a bowl. The name *Maiasaura* means "good mother lizard."

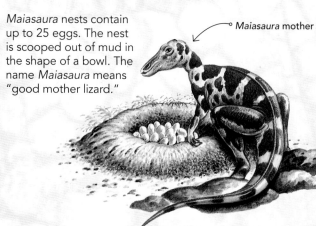

Maiasaura mother

FEEDING TIME

An adult *Oviraptor* brings food to its hatchlings. This meal could be a lizard or a young plant-eating dinosaur. A young *Oviraptor* is too small to hunt anything except insects.

Nest made of leaves and twigs

RAISING A FAMILY

Some plant-eaters care for their newly hatched young for weeks until they can walk. During that time, the hatchlings depend entirely on their parents for food and for protection from predators. Small, meat-eating dinosaurs grow more quickly and can probably run soon after hatching.

Baby dinosaur caught by mother

LIVING IN HERDS

Some plant-eating dinosaurs, such as sauropods, hadrosaurs, and ceratopsians, lived in herds. This helped protect their young from preying meat-eaters. Scientists have found fossilized footprints, known as trackways, that show meat-eating dinosaurs following herds of plant-eaters. If young, sick, or weak animals became isolated from the group, they were vulnerable to attack. They were a good source of food —one sauropod could feed a number of meat-eaters for a week.

Sauropod

PROTECTING THE YOUNG

Triceratops is probably the most common dinosaur in North America during the Late Cretaceous period. It lives in large herds, and adults form a protective ring around their young when threatened. *Triceratops* is not a fast mover, but its skull is extra thick at the base of its horns and is strong enough to ram the legs of a tyrannosaur.

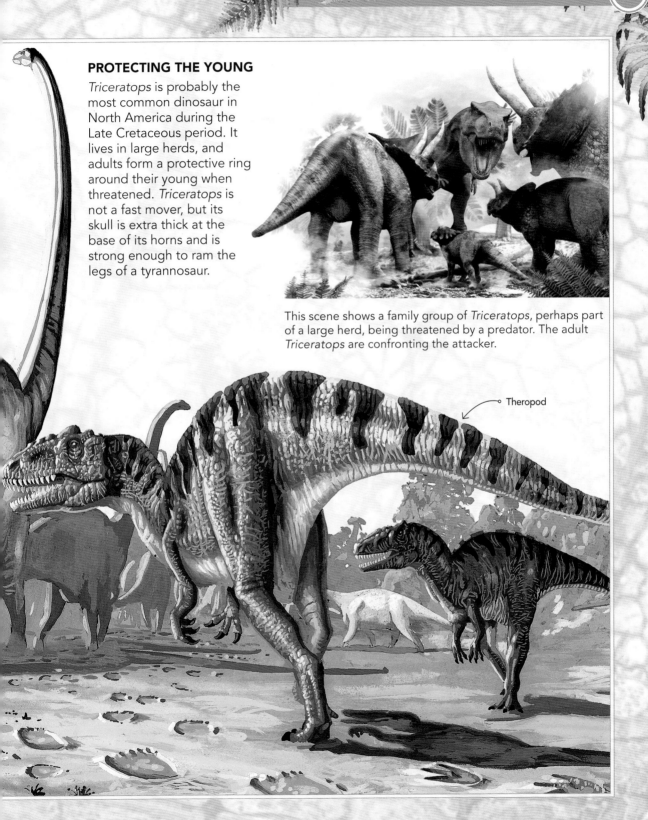

This scene shows a family group of *Triceratops*, perhaps part of a large herd, being threatened by a predator. The adult *Triceratops* are confronting the attacker.

Theropod

PREDATORS AND SCAVENGERS

There were three ways meat-eating dinosaurs could get a meal. They could find one, steal one, or kill one. Most meat-eaters were both predators and scavengers. It was easier and safer to scavenge a carcass or finish off a dying animal than to hunt and kill a live one. A large carcass could feed many animals. When the biggest and strongest predators had finished eating, the smaller scavengers fought over the leftovers. Even small animals, such as birds and young dinosaurs, could find something to eat on a carcass.

EGG THIEF

The name *Oviraptor* means "egg thief," because scientists thought it stole and maybe ate the eggs of other dinosaurs. Scientists now think these "stolen" eggs were actually *Oviraptor*'s own, which the dinosaur cared for itself.

Oviraptor

NO WAY!

Meat-eating dinosaurs do not chew their food. They swallow bite-sized pieces whole —bones, skin, feet, and scales.

Deinonychus

A CRETACEOUS BATTLE

A number of *Deinonychus*, meat-eating theropods, which may have had longer feathers, attack a *Tenontosaurus*, an ornithopod. One theropod has been trampled and will soon die from its injuries. The rest go for *Tenontosaurus'* neck and body, its least defended parts. This scene is based on information gathered from a fossil site in the USA.

Tenontosaurus

JURASSIC OPPORTUNISTS

A *Camptosaurus* lies dead by a river. Young *Allosaurus* are attracted by the scent. They will use their foot claws to open the thick skin and feed while they can before the adult *Allosaurus* show up to take the carcass from them. Insects on the body also become a quick snack for the opportunistic dinosaurs.

SURVIVAL TECHNIQUES

Dinosaurs had to survive in a world full of dangers. They had to find enough food to eat and, at the same time, protect themselves from being eaten. Plant-eaters were better defenders than meat-eaters. They protected themselves with horns, armour and spikes – and by living in herds. Meat-eaters needed to capture their food. They used claws and teeth to kill their prey. When meat-eaters were attacked they used their speed, claws and teeth for defence.

NO WAY!

Very large predators injure themselves if they fall. If a *Tyrannosaurus* trips while running at 20km/h, it crushes its rib cage.

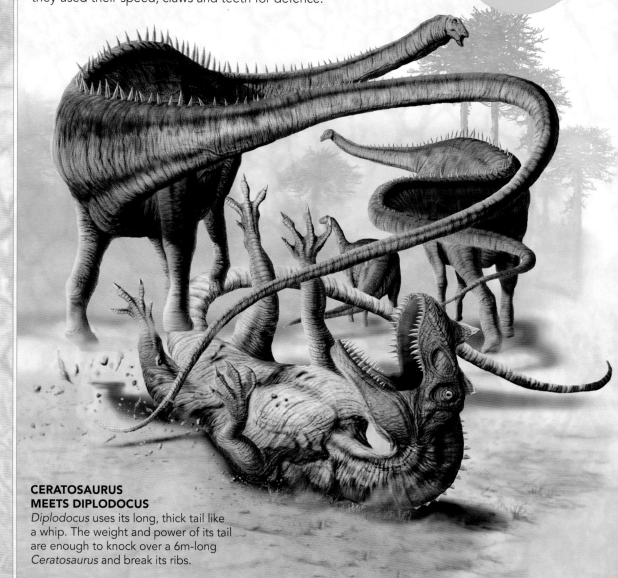

CERATOSAURUS MEETS DIPLODOCUS
Diplodocus uses its long, thick tail like a whip. The weight and power of its tail are enough to knock over a 6m-long *Ceratosaurus* and break its ribs.

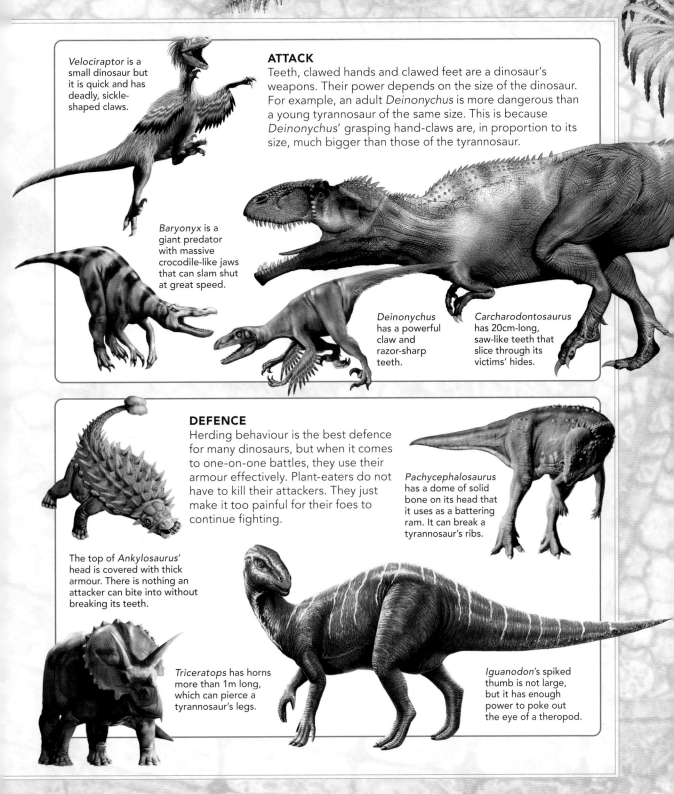

Velociraptor is a small dinosaur but it is quick and has deadly, sickle-shaped claws.

ATTACK

Teeth, clawed hands and clawed feet are a dinosaur's weapons. Their power depends on the size of the dinosaur. For example, an adult *Deinonychus* is more dangerous than a young tyrannosaur of the same size. This is because *Deinonychus'* grasping hand-claws are, in proportion to its size, much bigger than those of the tyrannosaur.

Baryonyx is a giant predator with massive crocodile-like jaws that can slam shut at great speed.

Deinonychus has a powerful claw and razor-sharp teeth.

Carcharodontosaurus has 20cm-long, saw-like teeth that slice through its victims' hides.

DEFENCE

Herding behaviour is the best defence for many dinosaurs, but when it comes to one-on-one battles, they use their armour effectively. Plant-eaters do not have to kill their attackers. They just make it too painful for their foes to continue fighting.

Pachycephalosaurus has a dome of solid bone on its head that it uses as a battering ram. It can break a tyrannosaur's ribs.

The top of *Ankylosaurus'* head is covered with thick armour. There is nothing an attacker can bite into without breaking its teeth.

Triceratops has horns more than 1m long, which can pierce a tyrannosaur's legs.

Iguanodon's spiked thumb is not large, but it has enough power to poke out the eye of a theropod.

SIZE AND SPEED

There are certain things that happen to all animals as they get bigger. The heavier they become, the more energy they need to move. Also, the larger the animal, the more they hurt themselves if they fall down. It also gets harder for them to cool down when they move quickly. Two-legged animals are smaller than four-legged animals because two legs cannot bear as much weight as four legs can. Above a certain size, four-legged animals can walk, but can no longer run.

FAST RUNNING

There is a simple way to tell how fast a dinosaur can run. If its thighbone is shorter than the rest of its leg bones, then it is fast. Also, if the thighbone has bumps and knobs for the insertion of muscles, then it has powerful legs and is a good runner.

The legs of an ostrich are built for speed. It can run at up to 70km/h.

Struthiomimus is not as speedy as an ostrich, but it can outrun a tyrannosaur.

BIGGEST PREDATOR

There are many competitors for the crown of biggest predator, including *Spinosaurus*, *Giganotosaurus*, *Oxalaia*, *Saurophaganax*, *Carcharodontosaurus* and *Bahariasaurus*.

LONGEST

The longest dinosaur is either *Barosaurus* at 38m or *Argentinosaurus* at 30–40m. New discoveries are helping to make measurements of these and other huge sauropods more accurate.

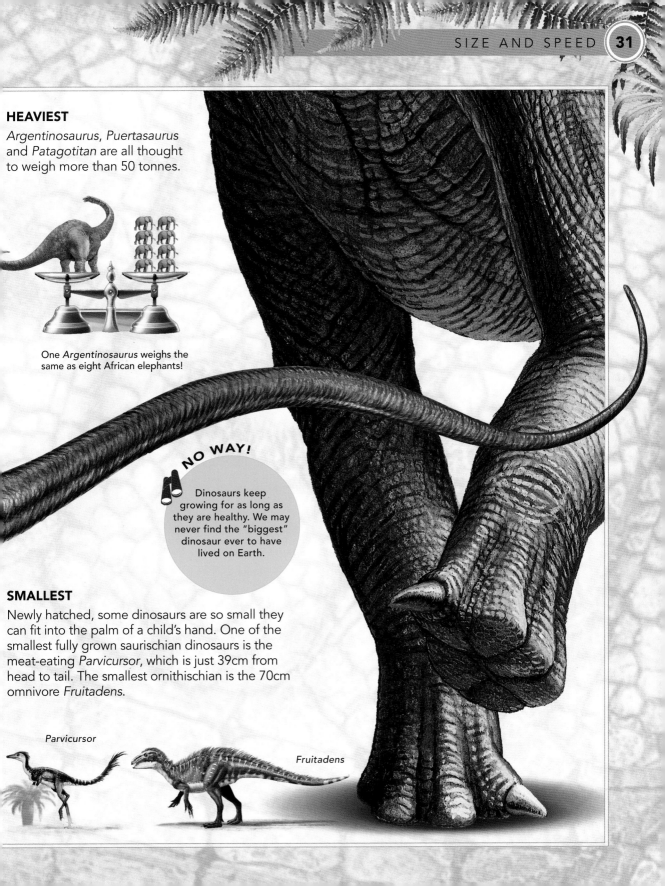

HEAVIEST

Argentinosaurus, *Puertasaurus* and *Patagotitan* are all thought to weigh more than 50 tonnes.

One *Argentinosaurus* weighs the same as eight African elephants!

NO WAY!

Dinosaurs keep growing for as long as they are healthy. We may never find the "biggest" dinosaur ever to have lived on Earth.

SMALLEST

Newly hatched, some dinosaurs are so small they can fit into the palm of a child's hand. One of the smallest fully grown saurischian dinosaurs is the meat-eating *Parvicursor*, which is just 39cm from head to tail. The smallest ornithischian is the 70cm omnivore *Fruitadens*.

Parvicursor

Fruitadens

ARMOUR AND DEFENCE

Ornithischian ("bird-hipped") dinosaurs were primarily plant-eaters. They needed a defence against the faster meat-eaters. By the end of the Mesozoic era, they had evolved the strongest armour any animal has ever had. These defences included spikes on stegosaurs and ceratopsians, armour on ankylosaurs, plates on stegosaurs, and small bone patches in the skin – osteoderms – which all ornithischians seem to have had.

NO WAY!

All these dinosaurs' defences may be covered by horn to make them sharper and longer.

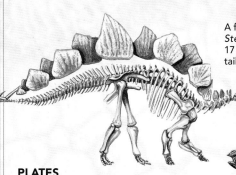

A fully grown *Stegosaurus* has 17 plates and four tail spikes.

PLATES
Stegosaurus is armed with plates along each side of its backbone, from its neck down to the middle of its tail.

The skin on the outside of *Stegosaurus'* plates may be able to change colour and act as a warning to potential predators.

BUILT FOR DEFENCE
The ankylosaur *Euoplocephalus* has armour, shoulder spikes and a tail club. Each armour plate is bite proof. To grow that much bone, ankylosaurs need lots of calcium. They may eat insects to supplement the calcium in their diet.

Euoplocephalus has armour fused to its skull. To make it lighter, there are eight cavities (holes) in its head.

The back armour is in strips, running from left to right, separated by bands of skin. This makes it flexible.

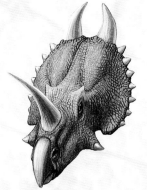

NASAL HORNS
Centrosaurine horned dinosaurs have nasal horns as well as frill spikes on a small frill shield.

BROW HORNS
Chasmosaurine horned dinosaurs have brow horns, fewer and smaller frill spikes and a larger frill shield.

TRICERATOPS

This fearless plant-eater will take on a *Tyrannosaurus rex*. Its cheek spikes protect its jaw muscles at the base of the frill, and can spear the leg of a tyrannosaur. The horns grow to more than 1m in length.

CLAWS AND SPIKES

Claws and spikes were mostly used for attack and defence. Dinosaur claws came in many shapes and sizes. They could be thin, thick, short, long, straight or curved. Foot claws were dangerous because they had a lot of muscle power behind them. Attacking hand claws would have been terrifying when a dinosaur reared up on its hind legs. The most effective spikes were ones that looked so scary they made a predator look elsewhere for a meal. Spikes that grew on the shoulder or the tail, and moved like spears, were used actively for defence.

CLAWED FEET
Utahraptor is a bird-like theropod with a 23cm, sickle-shaped claw on each foot. Its feet are its main weapons.

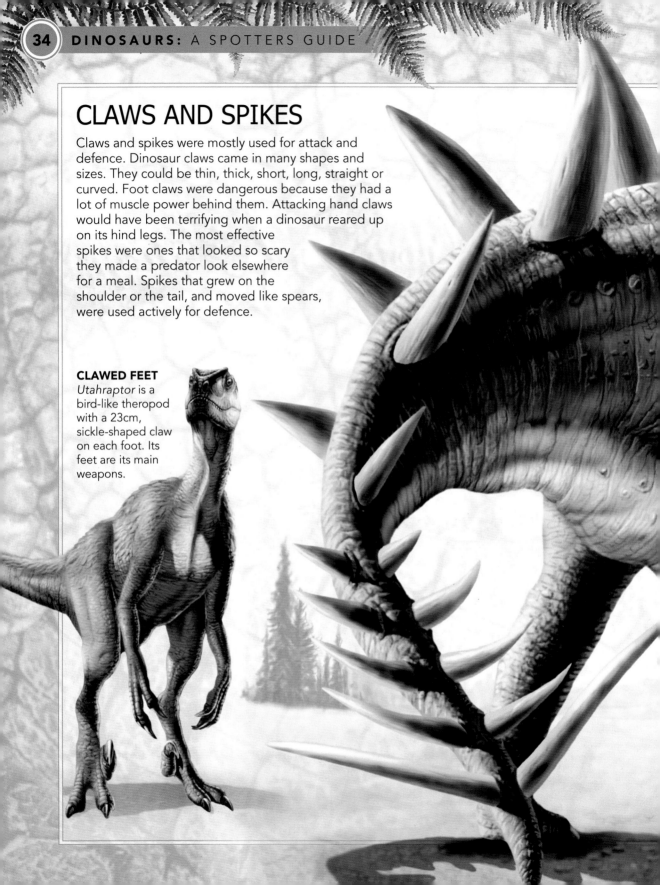

DEADLY DEFENCE

Dacentrurus, a stegosaur, is a moving fort. Its longest spikes can pierce deeply into a predator. *Dacentrurus* does not have to kill, it just has to disable. Its tail spikes are at the same level as the legs of a large predator. It only has to damage one leg of an attacker and the fight is over.

NO WAY!

Not all claws are for attack. The theropod *Mononykus* uses its claws to dig up termite mounds, as anteaters do today.

TEETH

Dinosaur teeth have two main parts: the root and the crown. The crown is made of hard enamel on the outside and a softer lining on the inside. Meat-eaters' teeth have long roots while plant-eaters' have short roots. Teeth are continually replaced throughout a dinosaur's life, which means that cavities do not have time to form.

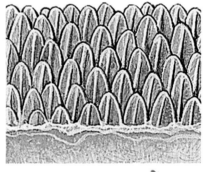

Crown

Different shapes
Plant-eating hadrosaurs' teeth (above) are interlocked. *Plateosaurus*' teeth (right) have bumps along the edges to cut through rough plant material. Theropod teeth (below) are like daggers, spaced apart so that they can cut meat.

Root

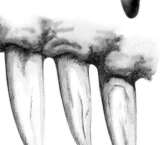

Sharp point

ABELISAURUS
ah-BEL-ee-SAW-rus

MEAT-EATER

LATE CRETACEOUS

DANGER LEVEL 5

Place to spot: Argentina
Habitat: Arid plains
When: 80 mya
Name means: After Roberto Abel
Alert: Powerful jaw

BIG SKULL
This dinosaur is part of a group of meat-eaters that evolved separately from the tyrannosaurs. Scientists have found a skull that is nearly 3 feet, but they do not know for certain how large *Abelisaurus* grew.

USEFUL TIP!

Stay out of this dinosaur's path. It attacks head-on!

Large, bluntly pointed scales

Slender lower jaw

Short forearms

Heavy tail

JAWS
Abelisaurus has a high skull and very powerful jaw muscles—its jaw can slam shut so fast that its prey does not have time to react.

NO WAY!

Abelisaurus has very large holes, called *fenestrae*, in its skull. These reduce the weight of its big head.

Large, weight-bearing toes

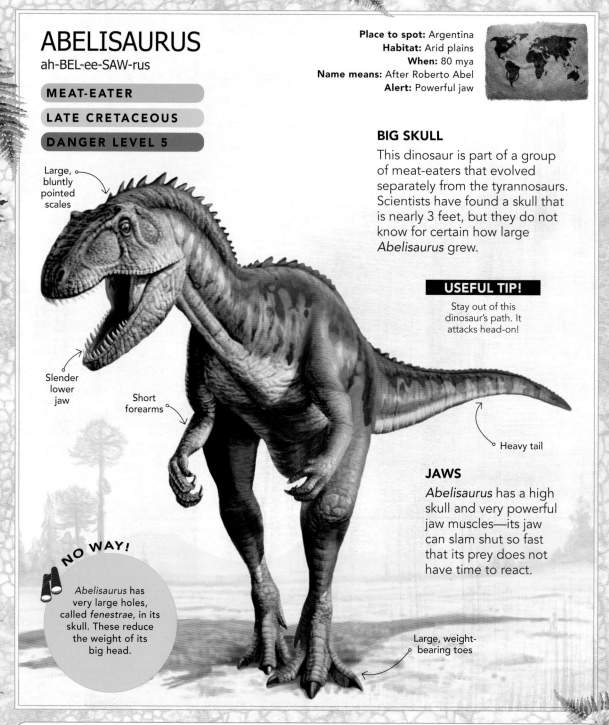

Length: 24 ft.
Diet: Meat
Group: Theropoda
Family: Abelisauridae

• *Abelisaurus* attacks young sauropods and medium-sized ornithopods headfirst. It also scavenges on carrion (the flesh of dead animals).

Place to spot: USA
Habitat: Woodland edges
When: 105 mya
Name means: Abydos (mythological city on the River Nile) lizard
Alert: Gigantic size

ABYDOSAURUS
ah-BY-do-SOR-us

PLANT-EATER

EARLY CRETACEOUS

DANGER LEVEL 3

Small head

Narrow teeth

Long neck to reach leaves

BIG EATER

Abydosaurus can't chew, so when its small head tears food from the trees, it swallows it all in one gulp. This lets the dinosaur eat more food at a time.

NO WAY!

Abydosaurus' skull is so tiny that it makes up only half a percent of the full weight of the dinosaur.

TINY TEETH

Abydosaurus has very narrow teeth compared to most brachiosaurs. This allows it to fit more of them in its mouth. Such small teeth wear down rapidly, but they are probably quickly replaced with new ones.

USEFUL TIP!

Stay well clear! This dinosaur may be a plant-eater, but it is big and heavy, and might be dangerous.

Length: 59 ft.
Diet: Plants
Group: Sauropodomorpha
Family: Brachiosauridae

• *Abydosaurus* eats by pulling leaves off shrubs and trees. These are then crushed against small pebbles, called gastroliths, in its stomach.

PROTECTIVE SPIKES

The horns on this centrosaurine protect its frill from being bitten by tyrannosaurs. Shaking its head from side to side moves the spikes like small pickaxes.

Place to spot: USA, Canada
Habitat: Forests and plains
When: 80 mya
Name means: Alberta (Canada) horned face
Alert: Dangerous horns

NO WAY!

In place of a nose horn, *Albertaceratops* has a bony ridge on its nose.

Hooks face sideways

Large frill

Short tail

Sharp beak

Broad feet

ALBERTACERATOPS
al-BER-ta-SER-a-tops

PLANT-EATER

LATE CRETACEOUS

DANGER LEVEL 3

USEFUL TIP!
May be found traveling in large herds.

EARLY CENTROSAUR

Albertaceratops lives more than 10 million years before *Triceratops*. It is one of the earliest known members of the centrosaur subfamily.

Length: 16 ft.
Diet: Plants
Group: Ornithischia
Family: Ceratopsidae

• *Albertaceratops* is known from one very well preserved skull from Alberta, Canada, plus other bones discovered in Montana.

Place to spot: USA, Canada
Habitat: Woodland
When: 70 mya
Name means: Alberta (Canada) lizard
Alert: Powerful bite

ALBERTOSAURUS
al-BER-to-SAW-rus

MEAT-EATER

LATE CRETACEOUS

DANGER LEVEL 5

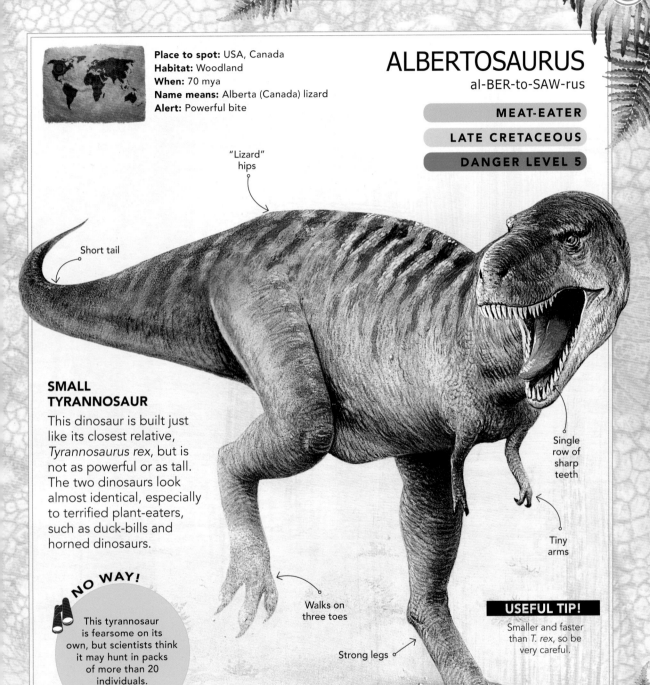

"Lizard" hips

Short tail

SMALL TYRANNOSAUR

This dinosaur is built just like its closest relative, *Tyrannosaurus rex*, but is not as powerful or as tall. The two dinosaurs look almost identical, especially to terrified plant-eaters, such as duck-bills and horned dinosaurs.

Single row of sharp teeth

Tiny arms

NO WAY!

This tyrannosaur is fearsome on its own, but scientists think it may hunt in packs of more than 20 individuals.

Walks on three toes

Strong legs

USEFUL TIP!

Smaller and faster than *T. rex*, so be very careful.

Length: 26 ft.
Diet: Meat
Group: Theropoda
Family: Tyrannosauridae

• *Albertosaurus'* jaws have just one row of teeth, but with replacement teeth below waiting to come through.

ALLOSAURUS
AL-oh-SAW-rus

MEAT-EATER

LATE JURASSIC

DANGER LEVEL 5

Place to spot: USA, Portugal
Habitat: Forests and plains
When: 153–135 mya
Name means: Other lizard
Alert: Large, saw-edged teeth

USEFUL TIP!

If you see this dinosaur, hide! It's a fast runner.

NO WAY!

Scientists found one *Allosaurus* skeleton with a hole in its tail where it was smashed by a *Stegosaurus* tail spike.

Tail outstretched for balance

Thick neck

Massive, powerful legs

Grasping, three-clawed hand

Very strong, three-toed foot

BIG BITE

Allosaurus has a massive skull and powerful jaws. It opens its mouth wide enough to take huge bites.

LARGE PREY

Allosaurus' size means that it can hunt stegosaurs, ornithopods, and even large sauropods.

Length: 26-39 ft.
Diet: Meat
Group: Theropoda
Family: Allosauridae

• *Allosaurus* has parallel ridges running along the top of its snout, serrated (saw-edged) teeth, and triangular horns in front of its eyes.

Place to spot: Argentina
Habitat: River valleys
When: 89–85 mya
Name means: Alvarez's lizard
Alert: Fast runner

FAST RUNNER

Not much is known about this dinosaur because scientists lack a complete skeleton, but we know it can outrun most other dinosaurs and can catch small prey.

NO WAY!

Even though it has long feathers on its arms and tail, these are too short to allow the creature to fly.

Long tail

Crest of feathers on head

Sharp, single-clawed hands

Slender, powerful legs

FEATHER FIND

This rare dinosaur is close to the group of meat-eaters most closely related to birds. Although it is from South America, it has features similar to those of the ornithomimids, or ostrichlike dinosaurs, of North America.

USEFUL TIP!

Alvarezsaurus' mouth has a powerful snap —so beware!

ALVAREZSAURUS
ahl-vahr-ez-SAW-rus

MEAT-EATER

LATE CRETACEOUS

DANGER LEVEL 2

Length: 6 ft.
Diet: Meat
Group: Theropoda
Family: Alvarezsauridae

• *Alvarezsaurus* has a small, birdlike head on a long, flexible neck, and large eyes on the sides of its head to spot danger from any direction.

ALWALKERIA

al-wah-KEER-ee-a

OMNIVORE

LATE TRIASSIC

DANGER LEVEL 1

WEIRD TEETH

This strange dinosaur eats both plants and meat. Its teeth are unusual—some are straight and others are curved. The most complete skull fossil that has been found is small. This may mean that the specimen is from the skeleton of a baby.

Place to spot: India
Habitat: Swampy plains
When: 228–220 mya
Name means: Alick Walker's lizard
Alert: Sharp claws

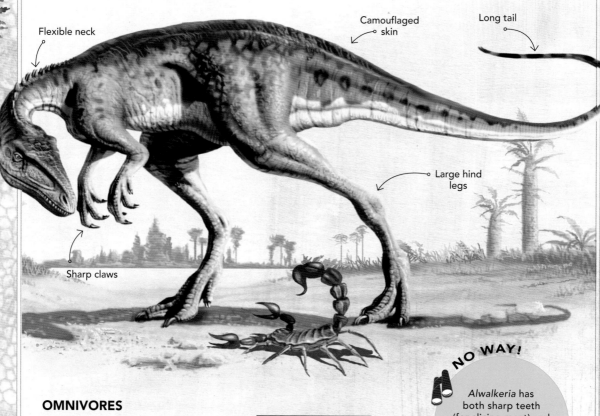

Flexible neck

Camouflaged skin

Long tail

Large hind legs

Sharp claws

OMNIVORES

Omnivorous dinosaurs are rare. They eat meat and plants, or whatever they can find, usually berries and seeds or grubs and insects.

USEFUL TIP!

Spot this dinosaur in swamps hunting for insects.

NO WAY!

Alwalkeria has both sharp teeth (for slicing meat) and blunt teeth (for chewing plants).

Length: 3 ft.
Diet: Plants and insects
Group: Saurischia
Family: Undecided

• *Alwalkeria* is probably a fast runner with good hearing and eyesight for spotting prey and avoiding predators.

Place to spot: Argentina
Habitat: Arid plains
When: 132–127 mya
Name means: Lizard from La Amarga
Alert: Double row of spines

USEFUL TIP!

Spot this dinosaur browsing ground-level plants.

MINI SAUROPOD

At only 33 feet long, this unusual dinosaur is small for a sauropod and has a shorter neck. It is unique for having two parallel rows of spines down its back and neck.

NO WAY!

One scientist thinks that *Amargasaurus'* rows of spines clattered together to make a sound display.

Tough skin covered in osteoderms —armorlike bony lumps

Spines are joined by skin

Sturdy tail for balance

Horselike snout

AMARGASAURUS
ah-MAHR-goh-SAW-rus

PLANT-EATER

EARLY CRETACEOUS

DANGER LEVEL 2

SPINES

Scientists are not sure what *Amargasaurus'* tall "sail" is for. It may be for attracting mates, to warn predators, or to help keep the dinosaur cool.

Length: 33 ft.
Diet: Plants
Group: Sauropodomorpha
Family: Dicraeosauridae

• *Amargasaurus* has a broad, horselike snout with pencil-shaped teeth for raking leaves from low-lying plants and low branches.

AMBOPTERYX
am-BOP-ter-ix

OMNIVORE

LATE JURASSIC

DANGER LEVEL 2

Place to spot: China
Habitat: Woodlands near lakes
When: 160 mya
Name means: Both wing
Alert: A nasty nip

Feathers cover
the neck,
shoulders,
and head

UNUSUAL ANIMAL

This theropod has strange rodlike bones that come out of its wrists. These may be to hold its wings. Unlike most theropods, it has a short tail and a pygostyle—a set of joined tail vertebrae—like a bird. Long feathers are attached to the tail.

Short tail

USEFUL TIP!

Look up into the treetops to see this odd little dinosaur.

Few teeth at
the front of
the jaw

Long third
finger

Batlike wings

Rodlike
wrist bone

LONG FINGER

Ambopteryx's third finger is very long, and was once thought to be for digging grubs out of rotting wood. It is now known to be for supporting the membrane of the wings.

NO WAY!

This small dinosaur's wings are made of membrane, similar to those of a bat.

Length: 1 ft.
Diet: Plants and perhaps meat
Group: Theropoda
Family: Scansoriopterygidae

• Although this dinosaur has stones in its stomach, which usually means it is a herbivore, bits of bone have also been found, suggesting it may also eat meat.

Place to spot: USA
Habitat: Forests, river valleys
When: 200–190 mya
Name means: Similar lizard
Alert: Sharp thumb claws

ANCHISAURUS
ANG-ki-SAW-rus

PLANT-EATER

EARLY JURASSIC

DANGER LEVEL 1

SMALL SAUROPOD

As one of the smaller and earliest sauropods, *Anchisaurus* is not as famous as the Jurassic giants. It weighs just 70 pounds and eats only ground-level plants. It has a thumb claw and blunt teeth. It is a slow walker and cannot outrun the meat-eaters.

NO WAY!

The gastroliths contained in *Anchisaurus'* gut help it grind up the plants it eats.

Long, flexible neck

Spoon-shaped teeth

Flexible spine

Long tail

Hands can turn inward for grasping

USEFUL TIP!

This sauropod is small enough to hide in ferns and other low-level foliage.

FOSSIL FOOTPRINT

Anchisaurus was the first dinosaur discovered in North America, in 1818. This footprint was found in sandstone in 1865.

Length: 6 ft.
Diet: Ground-level plants
Group: Sauropodomorpha
Family: Anchisauridae

• As such sauropods as *Anchisaurus* evolved into larger species, balancing on two legs became difficult, and their forearms became legs.

ANKYLOSAURUS
an-KEE-loh-SAW-rus

PLANT-EATER

LATE CRETACEOUS

DANGER LEVEL 3

Place to spot: Montana, USA
Habitat: Subtropical coastal plains
When: 70–65 mya
Name means: Fused lizard
Alert: Dangerous tail club

ARMOR-PLATED

Ankylosaurus' skull is covered in armor—imagine having a bone helmet fused to your skull! It cannot outrun a meat-eater, but it is a heavily armored tank that can stand its ground.

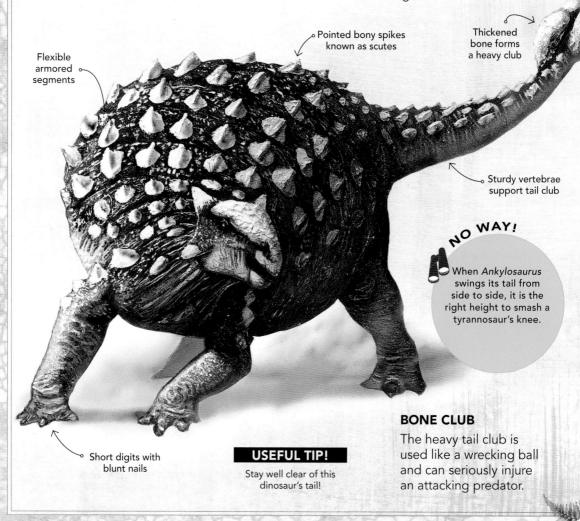

Flexible armored segments

Pointed bony spikes known as scutes

Thickened bone forms a heavy club

Sturdy vertebrae support tail club

NO WAY!

When *Ankylosaurus* swings its tail from side to side, it is the right height to smash a tyrannosaur's knee.

Short digits with blunt nails

USEFUL TIP!

Stay well clear of this dinosaur's tail!

BONE CLUB

The heavy tail club is used like a wrecking ball and can seriously injure an attacking predator.

Length: 26 ft.
Diet: Ground-level plants
Group: Ornithischia
Family: Ankylosauridae

• *Ankylosaurus* has a nasal passage with up to eight chambers. These help keep the animal cool, and allow a keen sense of smell.

Place to spot: Antarctica
Habitat: Conifer forests
When: 74–70 mya
Name means: Antarctic shield
Alert: Dangerous horns

ANTARCTOPELTA
ANT-ark-toe-PELL-ta

PLANT-EATER

LATE CRETACEOUS

DANGER LEVEL 3

BABY ANKYLOSAUR

The single fossil skeleton found of *Antarctopelta* is small, so it may be that of an infant or a small species.

Sharp, bony spike

Armor-plated with bony osteoderms

USEFUL TIP!

Be careful when you approach this dinosaur. It will turn its spikes toward you!

Sturdy tail

Bony spines

Toothless beak for cropping plants

NO WAY!

Antarctica during the Late Cretaceous was much warmer than it is today, and covered in deciduous forests.

Short, broad, three-toed feet

ANTARCTIC ISOLATION

Antarctopelta has body armor with many spikes. It is a late ankylosaur-like nodosaur that may have become isolated on Antarctica and continued to evolve there.

Length: 13 ft.
Diet: Ground-level plants
Group: Ornithischia
Family: Nodosauridae

• Like the earlier ankylosaurs, *Antarctopelta* has heavy armor, but scientists do not know from the fossils whether it has a tail club.

APATOSAURUS
a-PAT-o-SAW-rus

PLANT-EATER

LATE JURASSIC

DANGER LEVEL 3

Place to spot: USA
Habitat: Floodplains
When: 150 mya
Name means: Deceptive lizard
Alert: Gigantic size

Vertebrae form "suspension bridge" linking neck and tail

TAIL DEFENSE
Apart from its sheer size, *Apatosaurus'* whiplike tail may be used to swipe at predators.

Strong neck

Long, whiplike tail

Massive limbs supported by a fleshy pad

PLANT-MULCHER
This giant eating machine has a massive body. Its teeth are like the prongs on a rake, stripping leaves from trees. They swallow the leaves without chewing, then the food is mulched up in the gut.

USEFUL TIP!
Beware this dinosaur's swinging tail.

NO WAY!
Apatosaurus is one of the largest creatures that has ever walked on Earth. It weighs as much as six elephants!

Length: Up to 82 ft.
Diet: Plants
Group: Sauropodomorpha
Family: Diplodocidae

• Once *Apatosaurus* has reached adulthood, it is large enough to be safe from almost all predators.

Place to spot: Argentina
Habitat: Forests and plains
When: 90 mya
Name means: Argentina lizard
Alert: Gigantic size

ARGENTINOSAURUS
ah-jen-TEEN-oh-SAW-rus

PLANT-EATER

LATE CRETACEOUS

DANGER LEVEL 5

RECORD-BREAKER

Some scientists think *Argentinosaurus* is the largest animal to walk on Earth. Although only a few bones have been found, they include huge vertebrae up to 4 feet high. This dinosaur weighs about 55 tons and grows to a height of about 66 feet.

Small head

NO WAY!

Argentinosaurus' massive height means that it can look through a fifth-floor window of a building.

PATAGONIAN GIANT

Argentinosaurus lived in Argentina's southern Patagonia region, where nesting sites with thousands of football-sized eggs have been found.

Center of gravity near hips

Very long tail

Legs like massive columns

Massive hind leg

Short, stubby toes

USEFUL TIP!

Spot this animal's head rising above the trees.

Length: 115 ft.
Diet: Plants
Group: Sauropodomorpha
Family: Undecided

• To help reduce its weight, *Argentinosaurus'* immense ribs are hollow, cylindrical tubes.

AVIMIMUS

AY-vee-MY-mus

OMNIVORE

LATE CRETACEOUS

DANGER LEVEL 2

Place to spot: Mongolia
Habitat: Semiarid plains
When: 80–75 mya
Name means: Bird mimic
Alert: Very fast runner

BEAKED DINOSAUR

This lightly built, birdlike dinosaur is a type of oviraptor. It lives in semiarid conditions and eats plants and animals. It has a long neck and a beak with small teeth in the upper jaw.

NO WAY!

Avimimus may have many more feathers than pictured here, but it almost certainly cannot fly.

KEEN SENSES

Avimimus has large eyes and keen eyesight for spotting prey and avoiding predators.

Feathered arms

Short head

Tail may have feathers on it

Sharp claws

Long legs for speed

SPEEDY RUNNER

Avimimus is one of the fastest dinosaurs known.

USEFUL TIP!

Can be spotted chasing flying bugs.

Length: 5 ft.
Diet: Plants, insects
Group: Theropoda
Family: Oviraptorae

• *Avimimus* is one of several dinosaurs that probably evolved into today's birds. It may live in large flocks.

Place to spot: Montana, USA
Habitat: Open woodland
When: 84–71 mya
Name means: Bambi thief
Alert: Fast runner

BAMBIRAPTOR
BAM-bee-RAP-tor

MEAT-EATER

LATE CRETACEOUS

DANGER LEVEL 2

FEATHERED BODY

Bambiraptor belongs to a group of feathered dinosaurs—although no feathers were preserved with its fossil.

USEFUL TIP!

This specimen may be a youngster, so don't be surprised to see larger adults.

BIRDLIKE ARMS

What we know about this dinosaur comes from one fossil that is 95 percent complete. From this one specimen, scientists can tell that it has a large brain and that its forearms fold back against its body in the way a bird's can.

Birdlike
wrist joint

Feathered
arms

Feathered
tail

Deep snout
with sharp
teeth

NO WAY!

This dinosaur is named after the Disney animated character Bambi, because of its small size.

Raised claw for
making slashing kicks

Length: 3-5 ft.
Diet: Meat
Group: Theropoda
Family: Dromaeosauridae

• *Bambiraptor* is probably warm-blooded and covered in downy feathers that keep it warm. It is fast and active.

BAROSAURUS

BAH-roh-SAW-rus

- PLANT-EATER
- LATE JURASSIC
- DANGER LEVEL 3

Place to spot: USA
Habitat: Forests and plains
When: 156–145 mya
Name means: Heavy lizard
Alert: Huge and powerful

USEFUL TIP!

Likes to feed on tall trees.

STAYING COOL

The long neck helps *Barosaurus* keep cool in the hot summer.

LONG NECK

This Jurassic giant has a small head and small teeth. It eats soft plant material, which it reaches at the tops of trees with its long neck.

Thick neck

Spines embedded in skin

Long tail has more than 70 bones in it

Thick, relatively short legs

NO WAY!

This heavyweight weighs in at more than 22 tons—the same as three adult elephants.

Small head

LIVING WITH OTHERS

Barosaurus lives side by side with another giant, *Camarasaurus*, which specializes in tough plants and bark lower to the ground.

Length: 66-89 ft.
Diet: Plants
Group: Sauropodomorpha
Family: Diplodocidae

• In Late Jurassic North America, temperatures average more than 104°F in summer, dropping to 68°F in winter.

Place to spot: England, Spain and Portugal
Habitat: Near lakes
When: 130–125 mya
Name means: Heavy claw
Alert: Swift mover

CROCLIKE

This dinosaur lives along the shorelines and hunts in the water for fish. It has a long, slim neck and skull, and uses its slender snout to snap prey out of the water in the same way crocodiles do today.

BARYONYX
BARE-ee-ON-iks

MEAT-EATER

EARLY CRETACEOUS

DANGER LEVEL 4

USEFUL TIP!

Don't go near the water if you see this dinosaur nearby.

o Flexible neck

Crocodile-like
o skull

Powerful
arms o

NO WAY!

Baryonyx has 64 teeth—more than most theropods. The teeth are sharp and pointed to hold onto slippery prey.

o Huge claw

FISH-EATER

Baryoynx's thin jaw and finely serrated teeth are ideally suited to catching fish.

SHARP CLAW

Baronyx has a large thumb claw 10-14 inches long.

ARMS AND HANDS

The dinosaur uses its strong arms and big hands to hook prey from the water.

Length: Up to 31 ft.
Diet: Fish
Group: Theropoda
Family: Spinosauridae

• *Baryonyx* is bipedal and has been found with fish scales and bones in its stomach. It is one of the few known fish-eating dinosaurs.

NO WAY!

We don't know for sure what *Beipiaosaurus* eats. It may be an omnivore, meaning that it eats plants and meat.

PUZZLING FEATURES

Beipiaosaurus is a strange creature. It is a therizinosaur—a birdlike dinosaur with a long neck, a large head, and bulbous teeth, perhaps for eating plants rather than meat. Its body is covered with feathers, but it cannot fly.

Place to spot: China
Habitat: Forests and plains
When: 127–121 mya
Name means: Beipiao lizard
Alert: Dangerous claws

USEFUL TIP!

Bright feathers should make it easy to spot.

Longer feathers on neck

Large skull with cheek teeth

Sharp claws

Large feet

Small inner toe

BEIPIAOSAURUS

bay-pee-ow-SAW-rus

OMNIVORE

EARLY CRETACEOUS

DANGER LEVEL 2

MANY FEATHERS

This dinosaur has two kinds of hairlike feathers. Short, soft, downy feathers cover the whole body and probably keep it warm. Longer feathers on the arms and neck may be used for displaying to other *Beipiaosaurus* and for attracting mates.

Length: 7 ft.
Diet: Possibly meat and plants
Group: Theropoda
Family: Therizinosauridae

• *Beipiaosaurus* is one of the largest dinosaurs found that is known to have feathers, but what it uses them for is still a mystery.

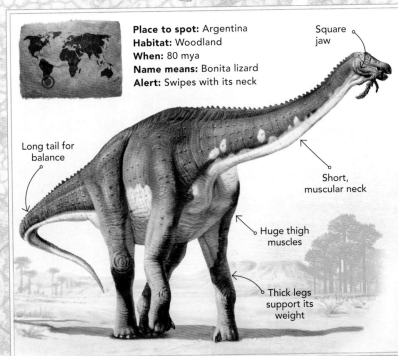

Place to spot: Argentina
Habitat: Woodland
When: 80 mya
Name means: Bonita lizard
Alert: Swipes with its neck

Square jaw

Long tail for balance

Short, muscular neck

Huge thigh muscles

Thick legs support its weight

BONITASAURA
bo-NEE-ta-SAW-ruh

PLANT-EATER

LATE CRETACEOUS

DANGER LEVEL 3

TREE-STRIPPER

Bonitasaura is a huge plant-eater with a wide mouth that looks a little like the front of a straight-edged shovel. It has lots of small, peglike teeth used to rake foliage from plants. With its short, powerful neck, it can tear branches from trees to reach their foliage.

Place to spot: Canada
Habitat: Scrubland
When: 112–110 mya
Name means: Northern shield
Alert: Spiky body armor

USEFUL TIP!

Can be seen searching the undergrowth for leaves and shoots.

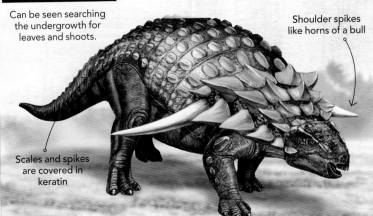

Shoulder spikes like horns of a bull

Scales and spikes are covered in keratin

BOREALOPELTA
boh-RAY-al-o-PEL-tuh

PLANT-EATER

EARLY CRETACEOUS

DANGER LEVEL 2

WELL ARMORED

This dinosaur has closely spaced rows of small armored plates along the top and sides of its wide body. A pair of long spines stick out from its shoulders, which give it good protection against predators, and may be useful in attracting a mate.

Length: 30 ft.
Diet: Plants
Group: Sauropodomorpha
Family: Titanosauridae

Length: 18 ft.
Diet: Mostly ferns
Group: Ankylosauria
Family: Nodosauridae

BRACHIOSAURUS
BRAK-ee-oh-SAW-rus

PLANT-EATER

LATE JURASSIC

DANGER LEVEL 3

Place to spot: USA, Tanzania
Habitat: Woodland
When: 156–145 mya
Name means: Arm lizard
Alert: Enormous size

GROWING TALL

This giant is tall enough to peek through the window of a five-story building, and it takes more than 30 years to grow this high. It is one of the few dinosaurs with front legs longer than its back legs.

NO WAY!

Scientists once thought that *Brachiosaurus* lived in water, using its long neck to stick its head out of the water like a snorkel.

USEFUL TIP!

Spends most of its time browsing on the leaves of tall trees.

Tiny head

Sloping back

Relatively short, stiff tail

30-foot-long neck

Long front legs

GIRAFFELIKE

Brachiosaurus stands in the same way as a giraffe. And, like the giraffe, it feeds on leaves from the treetops.

Length: 75 ft.
Diet: Plants
Group: Sauropodomorpha
Family: Brachiosauridae

• Weighing at least 33 tons, *Brachiosaurus* was once thought to be the heaviest dinosaur, but it has now been outweighed by other sauropods.

Place to spot: Mongolia
Habitat: Near lakes
When: 85–80 mya
Name means: Byron's lizard
Alert: Fast runner

BYRONOSAURUS
BY-ron-o-SAW-rus

MEAT-EATER

LATE CRETACEOUS

DANGER LEVEL 1

USEFUL TIP!

Lacking serrated teeth, this dinosaur poses little threat.

SMALL PREDATOR

This agile meat-eater can only attack small animals because it is slight, weighing just 10 pounds and standing 17-20 inches high. It has small, needlelike teeth.

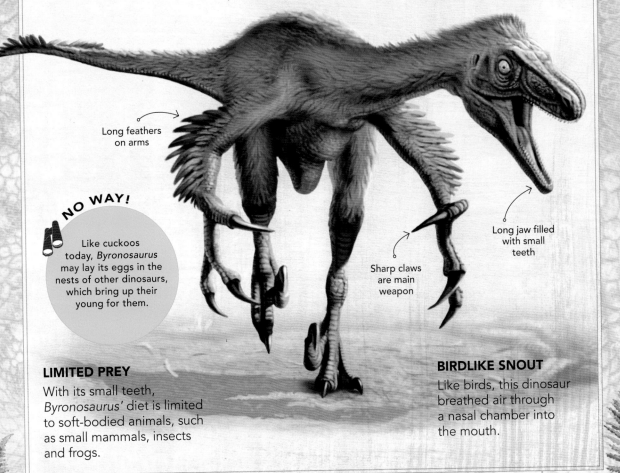

Long feathers on arms

NO WAY!

Like cuckoos today, *Byronosaurus* may lay its eggs in the nests of other dinosaurs, which bring up their young for them.

Sharp claws are main weapon

Long jaw filled with small teeth

LIMITED PREY

With its small teeth, *Byronosaurus'* diet is limited to soft-bodied animals, such as small mammals, insects and frogs.

BIRDLIKE SNOUT

Like birds, this dinosaur breathed air through a nasal chamber into the mouth.

Length: 5 ft.
Diet: Meat
Group: Theropoda
Family: Troodontidae

• The fossils of two adult *Byronosaurus* have been found, including one with a complete skull. Two skeletons of hatchlings have also been found.

CAMARASAURUS
KAM-a-ra-SAW-rus

PLANT-EATER

LATE JURASSIC

DANGER LEVEL 2

Place to spot: USA
Habitat: Forests and plains
When: 150–140 mya
Name means: Chambered lizard
Alert: Claw on front feet

NO WAY!
The dinosaur is named after the hollow spaces found in its vertebrae, which help reduce the weight of its skeleton.

STRIPPING TREES
This large plant-eater specializes in eating hard, fibrous vegetation. It uses its strong, 6-inch-long teeth to strip foliage from trees.

Square snout with large nostrils

Muscular neck helps it to strip branches

Thick legs

Thick tail

Inner toe has sharp claw

KEEN SENSES
The skull has a large nose cavity, which means that it probably has an excellent sense of smell.

USEFUL TIP!
Travels in herds, moving from place to place in search of food.

Length: 49-75 ft.
Diet: Woody plants
Group: Sauropodomorpha
Family: Camarasauridae

• *Camarasaurus* is one of the best-known sauropods, and its bones have been found all over western North America, including complete skeletons.

CARCHARODONTOSAURUS
kuh-KAR-oh-dont-oh-SAW-rus

MEAT-EATER

CRETACEOUS

DANGER LEVEL 5

Place to spot: North Africa
Habitat: Floodplains
When: 100–93 mya
Name means: Sharp-toothed lizard
Alert: Fast runner

USEFUL TIP!
Weighs up to
17 tons, but moves
very quickly for its size.

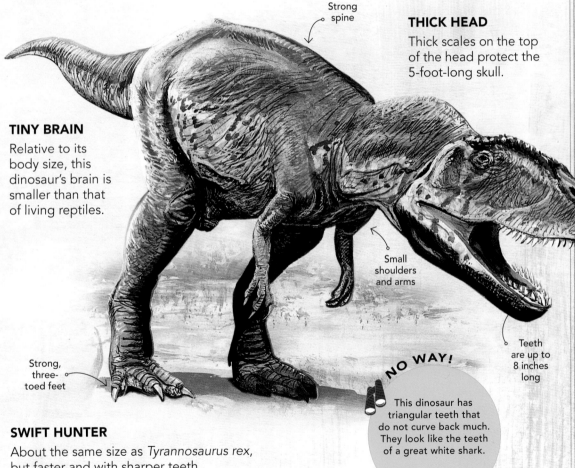

Strong
spine

THICK HEAD
Thick scales on the top
of the head protect the
5-foot-long skull.

TINY BRAIN
Relative to its
body size, this
dinosaur's brain is
smaller than that
of living reptiles.

Small
shoulders
and arms

Strong,
three-
toed feet

Teeth
are up to
8 inches
long

NO WAY!
This dinosaur has
triangular teeth that
do not curve back much.
They look like the teeth
of a great white shark.

SWIFT HUNTER
About the same size as *Tyrannosaurus rex*,
but faster and with sharper teeth,
this ferocious predator hunts sauropods
and other large plant-eaters.

Length: 43 ft.
Diet: Meat
Group: Theropoda
Family: Carcharodontosauridae

• *Carcharodontosaurus* hunts over huge ranges, and fierce
battles between rivals over territory are commonplace.

CARNOTAURUS

KAR-noh-TAW-rus

MEAT-EATER

LATE CRETACEOUS

DANGER LEVEL 5

Place to spot: Argentina
Habitat: Forests and plains
When: 72–66 mya
Name means: Meat-eating bull
Alert: Dangerous horns

AMBUSH PREDATOR

This small, slightly built meat-eater is one of the abelisaurs, a group of theropods common in the southern continents. It has two outstanding features: the horns above its eyes and its unusual forearms. It has a short skull and a weak lower jaw but can both attack large prey and swallow small prey whole.

NO WAY!

Its name means "meat-eating bull," referring to the horns that stick out above the eye sockets.

Narrow
skull

Sharp horns
on head

Skin covered
with rows of
bumps

Thick neck

Tiny
forearms

HORNS

Scientists are unsure about how *Carnotaurus* uses its horns. Some believe that they are just for show, while others think that they are used to wound prey and fight rivals.

USEFUL TIP!

Watch out for this hunter hiding in the foliage.

Length: 26 ft.
Diet: Meat
Group: Theropoda
Family: Abelisauridae

• *Carnotaurus* has a relatively small lower jaw with long teeth that can make rapid, powerful, and slashing bites on its prey.

Short, bony tail

Place to spot: China
Habitat: Near lakes
When: 125–122 mya
Name means: Tail feather
Alert: Fast runner

USEFUL TIP!

Probably spends a lot of its time hunting insects.

STOMACH STONES

Caudipteryx has swallowed stones, called gastroliths, which means it probably eats plants and animals—the gastroliths are used to help grind and digest plant matter.

Short head with sharp beak

Long feathers on wings

Powerful, spindly legs

NO WAY!

Even though it has long feathers on its arms and tail, these feathers are too short to allow the creature to fly.

BIRDLIKE

Caudipteryx has a mixture of reptile and bird features. Its long legs and light, hollow bones allow it to run at very fast speeds to chase down prey and avoid predators.

CAUDIPTERYX
kaw-DIP-ter-iks

OMNIVORE

EARLY CRETACEOUS

DANGER LEVEL 1

Length: 3 ft.
Diet: Meat, plants
Group: Theropoda
Family: Caudipteridae

• *Caudipteryx* is a feathered, birdlike dinosaur that cannot fly. Its discovery was the first to show that dinosaurs and birds are closely related.

NO WAY!

Centrosaurus skulls show differences that are probably those between males and females.

Place to spot: Canada
Habitat: Open woodland
When: 76–74 mya
Name means: Sharp-pointed lizard
Alert: Dangerous horns

USEFUL TIP!

It is very dangerous to approach. Don't make it angry!

Smaller, backward-pointing spikes on frill

Sharp horn

Hooked beak

Heavy tail

Blunt hooves

CENTROSAURUS
SEN-tro-SAW-rus

PLANT-EATER

LATE CRETACEOUS

DANGER LEVEL 3

HERD ANIMAL

Centrosaurus lives in large herds. Thousands of *Centrosaurus* skeletons have been found in one location in Canada. They may have drowned when a flash flood caught a herd crossing a river.

Length: 20 ft.
Diet: Plants
Group: Ceratopsia
Family: Ceratopsidae

• *Centrosaurus* has blunt hooves on its toes rather than claws, which helps this bulky animal grip the ground when walking.

Place to spot: USA and Portugal
Habitat: Scrub and woodland
When: 150–144 mya
Name means: Horned lizard
Alert: Fast runner

CERATOSAURUS
se-RAT-o-SAW-rus

MEAT-EATER

LATE JURASSIC

DANGER LEVEL 5

Short horn

NO WAY!

Males may duel with each other using their powerful arms by trying to push their opponent to the ground.

Bony ridges run along the back

Long, curved fangs

Deep, powerful neck

Short but powerful arms

JURASSIC PREDATOR

Ceratosaurus is a meat-eating dinosaur that lives at the end of the Jurassic period.

Long, clawed feet

THREATENING HORN

The horn on the end of *Ceratosaurus'* nose only appears on adults. It is too small to be an effective weapon, and is probably only used to display threat.

USEFUL TIP!

Not a fierce dinosaur, but stay away from its claws.

Length: 20 ft.
Diet: Meat
Group: Theropoda
Family: Ceratosauridae

• Only one complete skeleton of *Ceratosaurus* has been found. The specimen may not have been an adult, so this dinosaur may grow longer than 20 feet.

CHASMOSAURUS

KAS-mo-SAW-rus

PLANT-EATER

LATE CRETACEOUS

DANGER LEVEL 3

Places to spot: USA, Canada
Habitat: Forests and plains
When: 75 mya
Name means: Wide-opening lizard
Alert: Dangerous horns

THREE HORNS

Chasmosaurus is closely related to *Triceratops*. It has three horns on its head. A large frill at the back of its head balances out the weight of the horns.

USEFUL TIP!

If the frill is used for display, it will be bright and colorful.

SLOW MOVER

With a heavy body and short legs, *Chasmosaurus* is slow moving, but it has great stamina for long journeys.

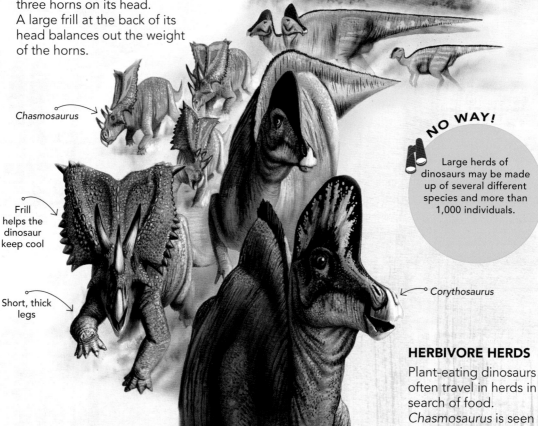

Chasmosaurus

Frill helps the dinosaur keep cool

Short, thick legs

NO WAY!

Large herds of dinosaurs may be made up of several different species and more than 1,000 individuals.

Corythosaurus

HERBIVORE HERDS

Plant-eating dinosaurs often travel in herds in search of food. *Chasmosaurus* is seen here with the crested *Corythosaurus*.

Length: 13-16 ft.
Diet: Plants
Group: Ceratopsia
Family: Ceratopsidae

• The skull of *Chasmosaurus* has a long snout and parrotlike beak. The frill bones contain two large holes, which probably have skin stretched over them.

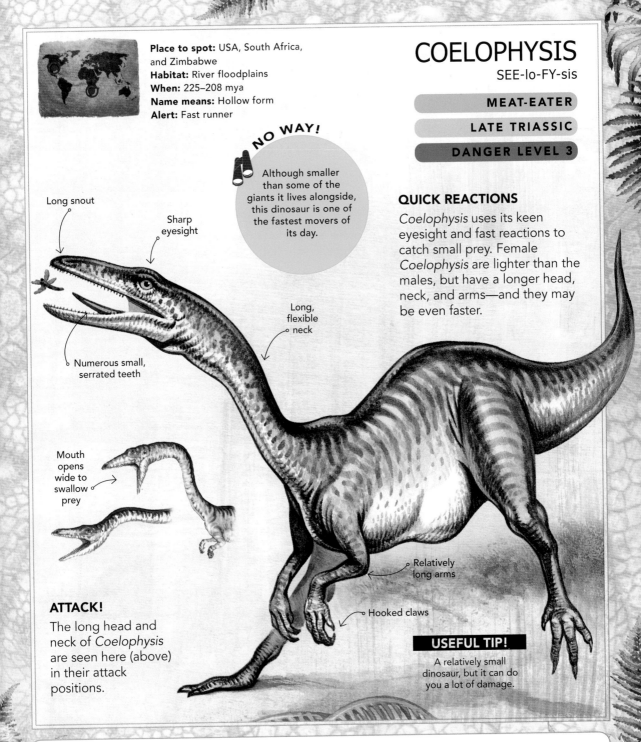

Place to spot: USA, South Africa, and Zimbabwe
Habitat: River floodplains
When: 225–208 mya
Name means: Hollow form
Alert: Fast runner

NO WAY!

Although smaller than some of the giants it lives alongside, this dinosaur is one of the fastest movers of its day.

COELOPHYSIS
SEE-lo-FY-sis

MEAT-EATER

LATE TRIASSIC

DANGER LEVEL 3

QUICK REACTIONS

Coelophysis uses its keen eyesight and fast reactions to catch small prey. Female *Coelophysis* are lighter than the males, but have a longer head, neck, and arms—and they may be even faster.

Long snout

Sharp eyesight

Long, flexible neck

Numerous small, serrated teeth

Mouth opens wide to swallow prey

Relatively long arms

Hooked claws

ATTACK!

The long head and neck of *Coelophysis* are seen here (above) in their attack positions.

USEFUL TIP!

A relatively small dinosaur, but it can do you a lot of damage.

Length: 10 ft.
Diet: Meat
Group: Theropoda
Family: Coelophysidae

• *Coelophysis* lives in herds and is known from many skeletons. It was found alongside small lizards, which are probably its prey.

COMPSOGNATHUS
KOMP-sog-NA-thus

MEAT-EATER

LATE JURASSIC

DANGER LEVEL 1

Place to spot: France, Germany
Habitat: Near lakes and coasts
When: 150 mya
Name means: Elegant jaw
Alert: Small and elusive

USEFUL TIP!

Little *Compsognathus* will probably be more scared of you than you will be of it.

Long, narrow head

Scales

LIGHTWEIGHT

Compsognathus has thin, light bones, which allow it to move around very quickly.

Arm bones

Leg bones

First claws used for grasping prey

NO WAY!

One *Compsognathus* was discovered with its last meal—a complete lizard—inside its stomach.

Long, stiff tail

Strong hind claws

Long, slim toes

DOWN IN ONE

Compsognathus is about the size of a large turkey, and preys on small animals that it swallows whole. Its teeth are adapted for grabbing prey, but not for slicing them up, as the teeth of many larger dinosaurs are.

Length: 3 ft.
Diet: Meat
Group: Theropoda
Family: Compsognathidae

• *Compsognathus* was found in the same fossil deposits as the first bird, *Archaeopteryx*, and the first pterosaurs.

Place to spot: Canada
Habitat: Near lakes and coasts
When: 80–65 mya
Name means: Corinthian helmet lizard
Alert: Fast runner

USEFUL TIP!

Listen for the dinosaurs' trumpetlike calls.

NO WAY!

The dinosaur's crest has two hollow chambers, which probably help it to control its temperature and humidity.

MAKING A CALL

This dinosaur's most distinctive feature is the bony crest on the top of its head. *Corythosaurus* may use this crest to make noises and communicate with others in the herd.

Heavy body

Crest and skull shaped a bit like a French horn

Toothless beak

Back legs longer than front legs

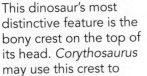

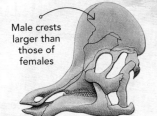

Male crests larger than those of females

SHOWING OFF

Males may use their tall crest to attract females and to intimidate other males.

CORYTHOSAURUS
ko-RITH-o-SAW-rus

PLANT-EATER

LATE CRETACEOUS

DANGER LEVEL 2

Length: 33 ft.
Diet: Plants
Group: Ornithopoda
Family: Hadrosauridae

• The first *Corythosaurus* specimen found was particularly remarkable because some of the skin had been preserved along with the bones.

CRYOLOPHOSAURUS
KRY-oh-loh-foh-SAW-rus

MEAT-EATER

EARLY JURASSIC

DANGER LEVEL 5

Place to spot: Antarctica
Habitat: Temperate plains
When: 199–191 mya
Name means: Frozen crested lizard
Alert: Comblike crest

SOUTH POLE DINO

This early Jurassic theropod was discovered 400 miles from the South Pole, at about 13,000 feet above sea level. Palaeontologists risked their lives in extreme conditions to collect these bones.

Long, stiff tail

USEFUL TIP!

If you spot this animal… run! It eats mammals.

High, comblike crest

Center of gravity in the hips

NO WAY!

This dinosaur's nickname is "Elvis" because of the crest on its skull, which looks like Elvis Presley's hair.

Slender arms with three-clawed fingers

Three long, forward-facing toes

Length: 21 ft.
Diet: Meat
Group: Theropoda
Family: Dilophosauridae

• Weighing more than 1,100 pounds, *Cryolophosaurus* is the heaviest of the early Jurassic theropods.

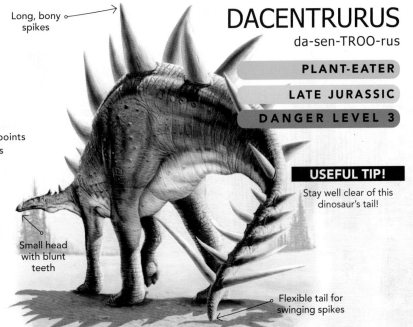

Long, bony spikes

DACENTRURUS
da-sen-TROO-rus

PLANT-EATER

LATE JURASSIC

DANGER LEVEL 3

Place to spot: England
Habitat: Near lakes
When: 154–150 mya
Name means: Tail with sharp points
Alert: Dangerous, sharp spikes

SPIKED BACK

This gigantic stegosaur lives at the same time as *Stegosaurus*. Both dinosaurs have long spikes and plates along their backs.

Small head with blunt teeth

USEFUL TIP!

Stay well clear of this dinosaur's tail!

Flexible tail for swinging spikes

Place to spot: Mongolia
Habitat: River deltas
When: 70 mya
Name means: Terrible hand
Alert: Slow, but big

Long, narrow skull

USEFUL TIP!

Keep an eye on the river—*Deinocheirus* may wade through the water to escape predators or get to food.

DEINOCHEIRUS
DY-no-KEY-rus

OMNIVORE

LATE CRETACEOUS

DANGER LEVEL 2

LUMBERING MONSTER

This huge dinosaur is much larger than other animals in its family, such as *Gallimimus*. *Deinocheirus* doesn't sprint. It lumbers along on chunky legs.

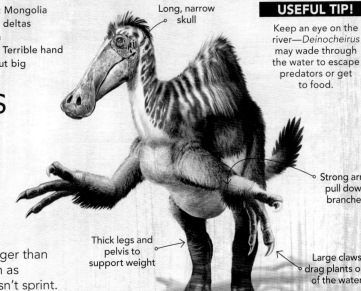

Strong arms pull down branches

Thick legs and pelvis to support weight

Large claws drag plants out of the water

Length: 20-26 ft.
Diet: Plants
Group: Stegosauria
Family: Stegosauridae

Length: 39 feet
Diet: Plants and possibly fish
Group: Ornithomimosauria
Family: Deinocheiridae

DEINONYCHUS
die-NON-ee-kus

MEAT-EATER

EARLY CRETACEOUS

DANGER LEVEL 5

Place to spot: USA
Habitat: Forests and plains
When: 115–108 mya
Name means: Terrible claw
Alert: Huge, slashing rear claw

SAVAGE CLAW

Deinonychus may not be very large, but it is a fearsome predator. The second toe of each rear foot has a razor-sharp, sicklelike claw. It uses this savage weapon, up to 5 inches long, to fatally wound its prey.

Good eyesight for spotting prey

Powerful jaws

Claws for ripping flesh

NO WAY!

Deinonychus' teeth act like a saw, cutting through skin, muscle, and bone.

USEFUL TIP!

Keep your distance —it's quick and deadly.

Large claw on second toe

SAWLIKE TEETH

It can deliver a ferocious bite with its 60 curved teeth.

KILLER CLAW

The claw can rotate quickly through 180 degrees.

Length: 8–10 ft.
Diet: Meat
Group: Theropoda
Family: Dromaeosauridae

• Studies of *Deinonychus* were the first to show that some dinosaurs were quick and agile, and that not all were cumbersome, as had been thought.

Place to spot: USA
Habitat: Forests near lakes and rivers
When: 80 mya
Name means: Devil-horned face
Alert: Dangerous horns

DIABLOCERATOPS
dee-AB-lo-SER-a-tops

> PLANT-EATER

> LATE CRETACEOUS

> DANGER LEVEL 3

HORNED DEVIL

Diabloceratops' huge head is a yard long from its beaked mouth to the back of its colorful frill. It is unusual for this type of dinosaur to have such long spikes above its eyes and curved, 20-inch-long devil-like horns on its frill.

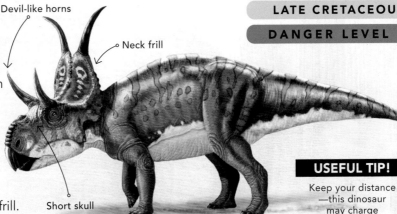

Devil-like horns

Neck frill

Short skull

USEFUL TIP!

Keep your distance —this dinosaur may charge without warning.

Place to spot: China
Habitat: Forests and plains
When: 125 mya
Name means: Emperor dragon
Alert: Fast runner

DILONG
dee-LONG

> MEAT-EATER

> EARLY CRETACEOUS

> DANGER LEVEL 3

USEFUL TIP!

A lone *Dilong* might not tackle a human —but a group of them might want to.

Short feathers on legs and body

Long, bright feathers for display

Snapping jaws for preying on small creatures

MINI REX

A small, feathered hunter, the flightless dinosaur *Dilong* is an early member of the tyrannosauroid family. This includes the much larger, and fiercer, *Tyrannosaurus rex*, which lives during the later Cretaceous period.

Length: 18 ft.
Diet: Plants
Group: Ceratopsia
Family: Ceratopsidae

Length: 6 ft.
Diet: Meat
Group: Theropoda
Family: Tyrannosauridae

DILOPHOSAURUS

die-LOF-o-SAW-rus

MEAT-EATER

EARLY JURASSIC

DANGER LEVEL 4

Places to spot: USA
Habitat: Scrub, open woodland
When: 201–189 mya
Name means: Two-crested lizard
Alert: Two strange crests

CRESTED HEAD

This lightly built theropod is not as tall as *Allosaurus*, but it is faster than most animals alive at this time. Its name comes from the two large semicircular crests on top of its head.

Dilophosaurus has a kinked upper jaw with a gap between its front and back teeth. These may help it to pull meat from carcasses.

Bony, semicircular crests

Long, slender teeth

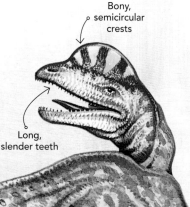

NO WAY!

The crests on *Dilophosaurus'* head may be so thin that sunlight passes through them.

Flexible tail

USEFUL TIP!
If you see a colorful crest moving through the foliage... run!

Length: 20-23 ft.
Diet: Meat
Group: Theropoda
Family: Dilophosauridae

• The male *Dilophosaurus* may nod its head up and down to show off its crests, either to attract females or to threaten rivals.

Place to spot: USA
Habitat: Floodplains
When: 154–150 mya
Name means: Double-beam
Alert: Whiplike tail

DIPLODOCUS
dip-LOD-o-kus

PLANT-EATER

LATE JURASSIC

DANGER LEVEL 2

Tiny head

BABY TEETH

A young *Diplodocus'* teeth are further back in the mouth than adults', suggesting they feed differently.

Long neck has 15 vertebrae

LONG LIZARD

At 100 feet long, *Diplodocus* is one of the longest known dinosaurs, with a 20-foot-long neck and a counterbalancing tail 20 feet long, with 80 vertebrae.

LEGS

Diplodocus' back legs are longer than its front legs. It can rear up onto its hind legs to reach leaves in taller trees or perhaps to scare off predators.

NO WAY!

Diplodocus feeds by gripping a branch with its peglike teeth and pulling its head sharply back, stripping the branch.

Front limbs short compared to hind limbs

BIGFOOT

Diplodocus' big feet carry its massive bulk. It walks on its toes, as an elephant does.

Length: 98 ft.
Diet: Plants
Group: Sauropodomorpha
Family: Diplodocidae

• *Diplodocus* gets its name from the "chevrons" in the bones of its tail, which may protect blood vessels when it rears.

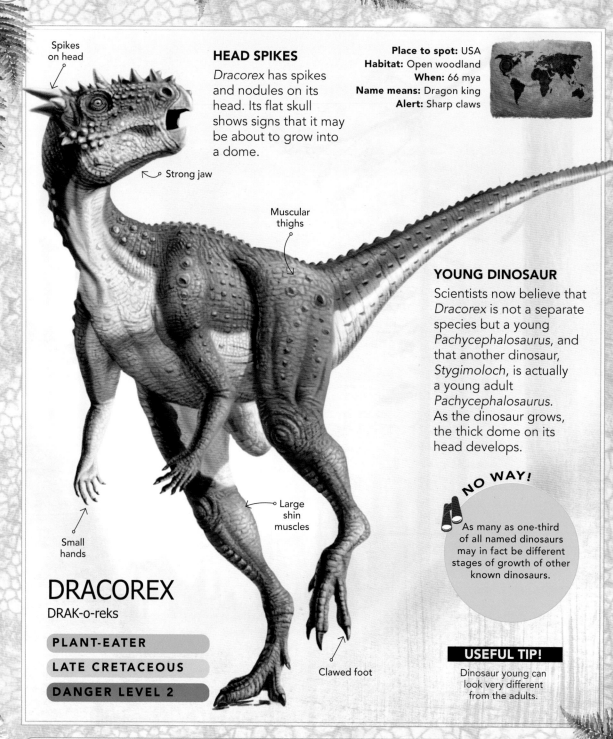

Spikes on head

HEAD SPIKES

Dracorex has spikes and nodules on its head. Its flat skull shows signs that it may be about to grow into a dome.

Strong jaw

Muscular thighs

Place to spot: USA
Habitat: Open woodland
When: 66 mya
Name means: Dragon king
Alert: Sharp claws

YOUNG DINOSAUR

Scientists now believe that *Dracorex* is not a separate species but a young *Pachycephalosaurus*, and that another dinosaur, *Stygimoloch*, is actually a young adult *Pachycephalosaurus*. As the dinosaur grows, the thick dome on its head develops.

Small hands

Large shin muscles

NO WAY!

As many as one-third of all named dinosaurs may in fact be different stages of growth of other known dinosaurs.

DRACOREX
DRAK-o-reks

PLANT-EATER

LATE CRETACEOUS

DANGER LEVEL 2

Clawed foot

USEFUL TIP!

Dinosaur young can look very different from the adults.

Length: Up to 13 ft.
Diet: Plants
Group: Pachycephalosauria
Family: Pachycephalosauridae

• The full name is *Dracorex hogwartsia*, after the wizard school in the Harry Potter books. It is known from one specimen discovered by three amateur dinosaur hunters.

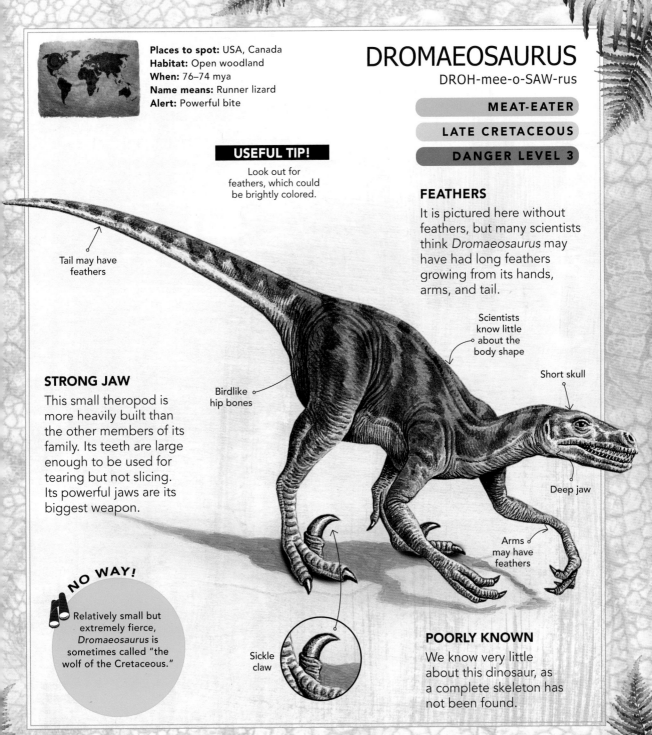

Places to spot: USA, Canada
Habitat: Open woodland
When: 76–74 mya
Name means: Runner lizard
Alert: Powerful bite

DROMAEOSAURUS
DROH-mee-o-SAW-rus

MEAT-EATER

LATE CRETACEOUS

DANGER LEVEL 3

USEFUL TIP!
Look out for feathers, which could be brightly colored.

FEATHERS
It is pictured here without feathers, but many scientists think *Dromaeosaurus* may have had long feathers growing from its hands, arms, and tail.

Tail may have feathers

Scientists know little about the body shape

Short skull

STRONG JAW
This small theropod is more heavily built than the other members of its family. Its teeth are large enough to be used for tearing but not slicing. Its powerful jaws are its biggest weapon.

Birdlike hip bones

Deep jaw

Arms may have feathers

NO WAY!
Relatively small but extremely fierce, *Dromaeosaurus* is sometimes called "the wolf of the Cretaceous."

Sickle claw

POORLY KNOWN
We know very little about this dinosaur, as a complete skeleton has not been found.

Length: Up to 6 ft.
Diet: Meat
Group: Theropoda
Family: Dromaeosauridae

• *Dromaeosaurus* is only known from a partial skull and a few bones from the hand and foot. Its skull is thick, and the rest of its skeleton may also be robust.

SMALL AND VULNERABLE

This plant-eater may grow up to be large, since known specimens are those of young animals. *Dryosaurus* is a lightly built dinosaur related to the iguanodonts, and its only defense is speed. With long feet and powerful hind legs, it can probably outrun any predators.

Place to spot: USA
Habitat: Dense forest
When: 150–145 mya
Name means: Oak lizard
Alert: Fast runner

NO WAY!

The inner toe on *Dryosaurus'* feet is missing. This allows it to run even faster.

USEFUL TIP!

This timid creature is likely to run off as soon as it sees you.

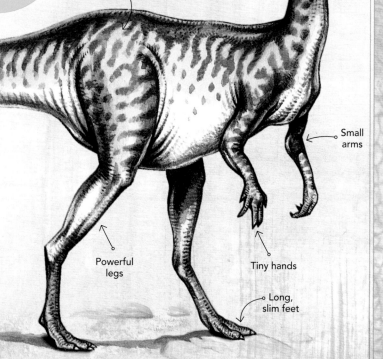

Narrow beak

Stiff tail is held out straight

"Bird" hip

Small arms

LEAF-EATER

Dryosaurus has a beak for snipping off leaves. Its teeth have leaf-shaped crowns to cut the leaves up in its mouth.

Powerful legs

Tiny hands

Long, slim feet

DRYOSAURUS
DRY-o-SAW-rus

PLANT-EATER

LATE JURASSIC

DANGER LEVEL 1

Length: 6–10 ft.
Diet: Leaves
Group: Ornithopoda
Family: Dryosauridae

• A fossil very similar to *Dryosaurus* has been found in Tanzania, East Africa. Further research shows that it is in fact a different species.

Places to spot: Canada, USA
Habitat: Woodland
When: 76–74 mya
Name means: Edmonton Foundation
Alert: Well protected

NO WAY!

Despite its body size, *Edmontonia* has tiny teeth. They are no larger than the teeth of a baby human.

HEAD PLATES

Interlocking bony plates protect the brain, eyes, and nose.

USEFUL TIP!

Slow-moving and not likely to be aggressive, it may freeze when it sees you.

METHANE MACHINE

Edmontonia has a narrow muzzle for picking and choosing its favorite plant foods. Its mobile tongue allows the food to be well chewed before it swallows. Further digestion in its large gut generates a large amount of methane.

Sharp spikes

Bony plate

SIDE WEAPON

The sharp shoulder spikes are an effective deterrent to potential predators.

Shoulder spikes

Thick legs

EDMONTONIA

ed-mon-TOH-nee-a

PLANT-EATER

LATE CRETACEOUS

DANGER LEVEL 2

Wide feet

Length: Up to 23 ft.
Diet: Plants
Group: Ankylosauria
Family: Nodosauridae

• *Edmontonia*'s belly is its most vulnerable area. In response to a threat, it may crouch to the ground, protecting its belly from attack.

EDMONTOSAURUS
ed-MONT-oh-SAW-rus

PLANT-EATER

LATE CRETACEOUS

DANGER LEVEL 2

Places to spot: USA, Canada
Habitat: Coastal plains
When: 76–65 mya
Name means: Lizard from Edmonton
Alert: Dangerous if provoked

BILL AND TEETH

Edmontosaurus is a noncrested duck-billed dinosaur. It has more than 720 interlocking diamond-shaped teeth. The teeth are constantly replaced as they wear out.

Nasal cavity

Teeth interlock

GRATER

The rows of tiny teeth in the back of the dinosaur's mouth act like a cheese grater.

Flat head

Horny bill

Strong spine

Slim arms

Thick tail

NO WAY!

In its lifetime, *Edmontosaurus* will grind its way through more than 10,000 teeth.

Feet with three hoofed toes

USEFUL TIP!

Look for plants less than 13 feet tall, and you may find these dinosaurs feeding.

Length: 39–43 ft.
Diet: Plants
Group: Ornithopoda
Family: Hadrosauridae

• Many *Edmontosaurus* fossils have been found. One fossil shows that the dinosaur died after an attack by a *Tyrannosaurus rex*.

Place to spot: USA
Habitat: Woodland
When: 84–71 mya
Name means: Buffalo lizard
Alert: Beware of the horns

HERD ANIMAL

Like the buffalo it is named after, *Einiosaurus* lives in herds. However, this dinosaur is much slower than a buffalo and is too heavy to run. Its downward-pointing nose horn is used both for defense and for display.

NO WAY!

The backward--pointing spikes on the dinosaur's frill appear to be of no use for defense. They may just be for display.

Backward-facing
spikes on frill

WIDE GRAZER

Einiosaurus has strong teeth, which allow it to graze on a wide range of plants.

Nose horn

Horny
beak

Armored
frill

Short tail

Thick
legs

EINIOSAURUS
eye-nee-o-SAW-rus

PLANT-EATER

LATE CRETACEOUS

DANGER LEVEL 3

USEFUL TIP!

Keep your distance from a herd of *Einiosaurus*.

Length: 20 ft.
Diet: Plants
Group: Ceratopsia
Family: Ceratopsidae

• Fossils of whole herds of *Einiosaurus* have been found together. The dinosaurs all died at the same time in a catastrophic flood or drought.

HEADBUTTING

This theropod has a prominent, bony eyebrow, and the roof of its skull is made of thick bone. This could mean that these dinosaurs butt heads during the mating season, as the males compete for the females.

Place to spot: Niger
Habitat: Open woodland
When: 112 mya
Name means: Dawn shark
Alert: Thick skull

NO WAY!

The bony growths above the eyes may be brightly colored to impress potential mates.

USEFUL TIP!

Stay away from that mouthful of teeth.

Short spikes on spine

"Lizard" hip

Tail held horizontal for balance

Relatively large arms

BLADELIKE TEETH

Eocarcharia, the "dawn shark," is named after its sharklike teeth. They are very sharp and can rip prey to pieces.

Strong legs

Three fingers

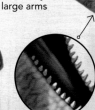

Serrated, bladelike teeth

EOCARCHARIA
EE-oh-car-KAIR-ee-a

MEAT-EATER

MID-CRETACEOUS

DANGER LEVEL 4

Length: 20–26 ft.
Diet: Meat
Group: Theropoda
Family: Carcharodontosauridae

• *Eocarcharia* is known from the remains of its head and teeth. Little is known about the rest of its body, which may have been up to 39 feet.

Place to spot: South Africa
Habitat: Woodland
When: 195 mya
Name means: Dawn runner
Alert: Small and fast

EOCURSOR
EE-oh-KUR-sore

OMNIVORE

EARLY JURASSIC

DANGER LEVEL 1

NO WAY!

Eocursor has long hands and sharp claws for grabbing plants and small animal prey.

SPEEDY OMNIVORE

Eocursor is a small, two-legged omnivore. Its leaf-shaped teeth are similar to those of the living iguana, adapted to feed on both plants and insects. Its shinbone is longer than its thighbone, which is a good indication that speed is its best defense.

USEFUL TIP!

Small, fast, and agile, *Eocursor* is hard to spot.

Thin tail

Narrow head

Eyes on side of head

Long hands

Flexible ankle

Long shinbone

Long toes

EARLY ORNITHISCHIAN

This is one of the most primitive of the ornithischian dinosaurs. It may be an ancestor of *Triceratops* and *Iguanodon*.

Length: 3 ft.
Diet: Plants and insects
Group: Ornithischia
Family: Undecided

• *Eocursor* is known from one of the best fossils of the early ornithischians, with a well-preserved skull, backbone, pelvis, arms, and legs.

EORAPTOR
EE-oh-RAP-tor

MEAT-EATER

LATE TRIASSIC

DANGER LEVEL 1

Place to spot: Argentina
Habitat: Forests
When: 232–228 mya
Name means: Dawn thief
Alert: Fierce for its size

NO WAY!
With its large, grasping arms, this fast-moving hunter may be able to catch prey almost as big as it is.

FIRST DINOSAUR?

This dog-size predator is perhaps the most primitive of all known dinosaurs. Some scientists think it is one of the first theropods, but it may also be an ancestor of the plant-eating sauropods.

Small head

May be camouflaged

Long tail

Large, five-fingered hands

USEFUL TIP!
Has a mouthful of sharp teeth, so don't let your guard down.

CLAWED HANDS

Eoraptor's arms have long hands with five fingers, three of which have large claws for grasping prey.

Length: 3 ft.
Diet: Meat
Group: Saurischia
Family: Undecided

• *Eoraptor* fossils were discovered in Argentina alongside the fossils of many other animals. At the time they were all alive, dinosaurs were outnumbered by other four-legged animals.

Place to spot: England, UK
Habitat: Open woodland
When: 127–121 mya
Name means: Dawn tyrant
Alert: Jaws and claws

EOTYRANNUS
EE-oh-ti-RAN-us

MEAT-EATER

EARLY CRETACEOUS

DANGER LEVEL 5

Flat skull

USEFUL TIP!
This formidable predator is not to be messed with!

LONG ARMS

Unlike its later relative *Tyrannosaurus rex*, *Eotyrannus* has long arms and hands with three clawed fingers for grabbing prey. It is also faster and more agile than *T. rex*.

Powerful thigh muscles

Small ornithopod

Fused wrist bone

Tail feathers

NO WAY!
Tyrannosaurus rex is nearly 100 times heavier than the earliest tyrannosauroids, such as *Eotyrannus*.

EFFECTIVE HUNTERS

By the end of the Cretaceous, nearly all large predators were tyrannosauroids, descended from smaller ancestors such as *Eotyrannus*.

Splayed toes

Length: Up to 13 ft.
Diet: Meat
Group: Theropoda
Family: Stokesauridae

• *Eotyrannus* has hollow bones, like modern-day birds have. This makes it lighter and faster.

PLANT-CHEWER

This plant-eating dinosaur is halfway between an iguanodont, such as *Iguanodon*, and the duck-billed hadrosaurs of the Late Cretaceous. Like later hadrosaurs, *Equijubus* has more than one row of teeth for grinding up its food.

FLEXIBLE JAW

Equijubus can move its jaw more than an iguanodont can, allowing it to chew its food.

Place to spot: China
Habitat: Woodland
When: 127–99 mya
Name means: Horse mane
Alert: Dangerous tail

Large eyes

Bill

Stiff tail

USEFUL TIP!

Can be spotted moving slowly through the foliage.

EQUIJUBUS
ee-kwi-JUH-bus

PLANT-EATER

EARLY CRETACEOUS

DANGER LEVEL 2

Sturdy legs

NO WAY!

Equijubus was found with grass inside of its body, the earliest known evidence for dinosaurs eating grass.

Length: 23–26 ft.
Diet: Plants
Group: Ornithopoda
Family: Undecided

• *Equijubus* is known from one fossil skull found in the Gobi Desert. Its discovery shows that hadrosaurs first evolved in Asia.

Place to spot: Mongolia
Habitat: Forest
When: 120 mya
Name means: Mighty deity
Alert: Huge size

ERKETU
err-KEH-too

PLANT-EATER

EARLY CRETACEOUS

DANGER LEVEL 3

Gray skin makes dinosaur hard to see

SUSPENSION NECK

Erketu's heavy body counterbalances the weight of its neck. Muscles in between its vertebrae hold up the neck—this same system is used in suspension bridges today.

USEFUL TIP!

Likely to be found grazing on tall trees.

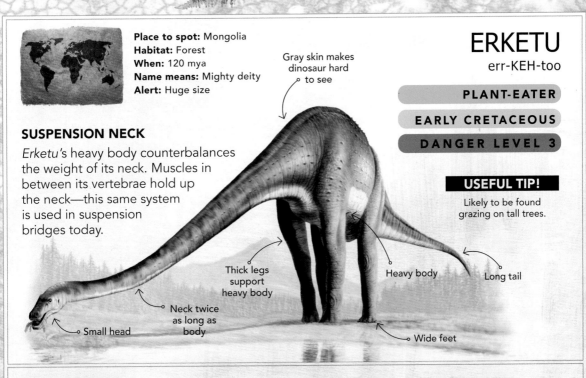

Thick legs support heavy body

Heavy body

Long tail

Neck twice as long as body

Small head

Wide feet

Place to spot: Brazil
Habitat: River deltas
When: 228 mya
Name means: Red hunter
Alert: Fast-moving with sharp, cutting teeth

ERYTHROVENATOR
eh-RITH-roh-VEN-uh-tor

MEAT-EATER

LATE TRIASSIC

DANGER LEVEL 4

Razorlike teeth

Binocular vision for spotting prey

Long legs for fast movement

LONE HUNTER

Erythrovenator can be found hunting alone, using its sharp teeth and claws to prey upon mammal-like reptiles called cynodonts. As well as eating small animals, this dinosaur scavenges larger carcasses. It is one of the oldest theropods we know about and might be the grandfather of *T. rex*!

USEFUL TIP!

Watch out! *Erythrovenator* has keen eyesight for hunting.

Length: 66 ft.
Diet: Leaves
Group: Sauropodomorpha
Family: Undecided

Length: 6 ft.
Diet: Meat
Group: Theropoda
Family: Undecided

EUOPLOCEPHALUS
yoo-oh-ploh-o-SEF-uh-lus

PLANT-EATER

LATE CRETACEOUS

DANGER LEVEL 4

Places to spot: USA, Canada
Habitat: Woodland
When: 76–67 mya
Name means: Well-armored head
Alert: Massive tail club

NO WAY!

Euoplocephalus can probably hear low-frequency sounds. Its nostrils may also make sounds.

HEAVY ARMOR

Euoplocephalus is a heavily armored, tanklike dinosaur. If surrounded, it simply drops to the ground so that only its bite-proof armor is visible, protecting its soft underbelly from attack.

Small spikes

Double-headed bony club at the end of the stiff tail

Vertical plates

Tail bones are fused together

Short, strong legs

Horny beak

Toes are tipped with a blunt hoof

USEFUL TIP!

Short and stocky, it is likely to be slow on its feet.

LETHAL WEAPON

The most lethal weapon in *Euoplocephalus'* armory is the double-headed club at the end of its long, stiffened tail.

Length: 20 ft.
Diet: Shoots and roots
Group: Ornithischia
Family: Ankylosauridae

• Armor plates on *Euoplocephalus'* head are outgrowths from the skull bones. Bony shutters in the eyelids protect its eyes.

Place to spot: Germany
Habitat: Woodland
When: 155–151 mya
Name means: Lizard from Europe
Alert: The size of a small elephant

EUROPASAURUS
yoo-ROPE-ah-SAW-rus

PLANT-EATER

LATE JURASSIC

DANGER LEVEL 2

DWARF SAUROPOD

Europasaurus is a dwarf species. Dwarfing occurs when animals are isolated on islands, where their food supply is limited. During the Late Jurassic, Europe was made up of several large islands about the size of Britain. The ancestors of *Europasaurus* became stranded on one of these islands, and evolved into this small sauropod.

NO WAY!

Europasaurus is the same shape as *Brachiosaurus*—but *Brachiosaurus* is more than 100 times heavier!

Arched head

USEFUL TIP!

May be hard to spot in the trees.

Neck is long compared to the rest of the body

Dull-colored skin

MUZZLE

Apart from its small size, *Europasaurus* is distinguished from other sauropods by having an unusually short muzzle.

Relatively short tail

Length: 20 ft.
Diet: Plants
Group: Saurapodomorpha
Family: Brachiosauridae

• The remains of 11 *Europasaurus* specimens have been found, ranging in size from 3-foot-long juveniles to 20-foot-long adults.

NO WAY!

This is the first dinosaur ever to have been discovered in Africa. It is one of the largest animals of its time.

Places to spot: South Africa, Zimbabwe, Lesotho
Habitat: Forests and plains
When: 227–210 mya
Name means: True-limbed lizard
Alert: May be aggressive

USEFUL TIP!

Can be seen feeding on the tops of small trees.

Long neck

Small head

LARGE PROSAUROPOD

Euskelosaurus is one of the largest and heaviest prosauropods. It is closely related to the first giant sauropod, *Plateosaurus*. *Euskelosaurus'* teeth can process both meat and plants, suggesting that this dinosaur may be an omnivore.

Thick, heavy body

LARGE GUT

The dinosaur's thighbones bow outward from its body, which makes room for a large gut for digesting tough plants.

Strong tail muscles

Long tail

Long arms

Hooked claw

EUSKELOSAURUS
you-SKEL-uh-SAW-rus

OMNIVORE

LATE TRIASSIC

DANGER LEVEL 3

Length: Up to 33 ft.
Diet: Plants and perhaps meat
Group: Sauropodomorpha
Family: Plateosauridae

• Prosauropods such as *Euskelosaurus* are common in the woodlands of southern Africa, and many fossils have been found in that region.

Place to spot: England
Habitat: Near shorelines
When: 165–161 mya
Name means: Well-curved vertebra
Alert: Good swimmer

EUSTREPTOSPONDYLUS
yoo-STREP-toh-SPON-die-lus

MEAT-EATER

MID-JURASSIC

DANGER LEVEL 3

USEFUL TIP!

This dinosaur swims much faster than you, so be careful in the water.

Skin may be camouflaged

SHORE HUNTER

Eustreptospondylus has a narrow, crocodile-like jaw—and, as with crocodiles, it is never far from water. It hunts along the shoreline and around lagoons and small islands, scavenging and foraging for marine life, such as fish and turtles.

Stiffened tail

WATERY GRAVE

The fossil of this dinosaur was found in marine clays. Its body was probably washed out to sea soon after it died.

Long, narrow jaw

Three clawed fingers on each hand

Powerful legs

NO WAY!

This theropod may be able to wade through shallow lagoons and marshes in search of food.

Clawed toes

Length: 13–23 ft.
Diet: Marine animals
Group: Theropoda
Family: Megalosauridae

• *Eustreptospondylus* is known from just one juvenile specimen. The adults may have grown to be considerably larger.

FALCARIUS
fal-KAIR-ree-us

OMNIVORE

EARLY CRETACEOUS

DANGER LEVEL 2

Place to spot: USA
Habitat: Woodland
When: 128 mya
Name means: Sickle-cutter
Alert: Long claws

HEAVY AND SLOW

Falcarius is a slowmover and will stand and fight an attacker rather than run away.

PLANT- OR MEAT-EATER?

This is an early therizinosaur—one of a bizarre group of plant-eaters that evolved from the meat-eating theropods and combines features of both groups. *Falcarius* has the wide hips, leaf-shaped teeth, and long neck of a plant-eater. It also has 5-inch-long sicklelike claws, a two-legged posture, and feathers like a meat-eater.

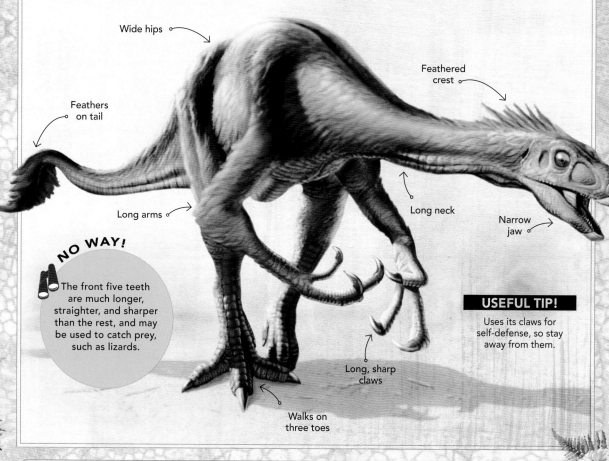

Wide hips

Feathered crest

Feathers on tail

Long neck

Narrow jaw

Long arms

NO WAY!

The front five teeth are much longer, straighter, and sharper than the rest, and may be used to catch prey, such as lizards.

Long, sharp claws

USEFUL TIP!

Uses its claws for self-defense, so stay away from them.

Walks on three toes

Length: 13 ft.
Diet: Plants and perhaps meat
Group: Theropoda
Family: Undecided

• Since 1999, nearly 3,000 specimens of *Falcarius* have been uncovered in one location in the Cedar Mountain Formation in Utah.

Place to spot: Japan
Habitat: Forests and plains
When: 128 mya
Name means: Fukui thief
Alert: Fast and agile

FUKUIRAPTOR
foo-KOO-ee-RAP-tor

MEAT-EATER

EARLY CRETACEOUS

DANGER LEVEL 4

LATECOMER

This Cretaceous killer is related to a group of dinosaurs that lived mostly in the Jurassic period.

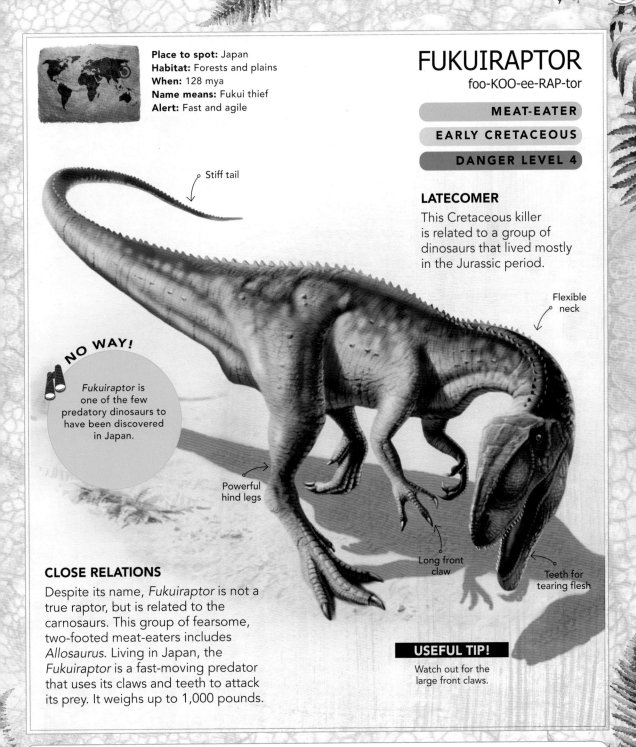

Stiff tail

Flexible neck

NO WAY!

Fukuiraptor is one of the few predatory dinosaurs to have been discovered in Japan.

Powerful hind legs

Long front claw

Teeth for tearing flesh

CLOSE RELATIONS

Despite its name, *Fukuiraptor* is not a true raptor, but is related to the carnosaurs. This group of fearsome, two-footed meat-eaters includes *Allosaurus*. Living in Japan, the *Fukuiraptor* is a fast-moving predator that uses its claws and teeth to attack its prey. It weighs up to 1,000 pounds.

USEFUL TIP!

Watch out for the large front claws.

Length: 15 ft.
Diet: Meat
Group: Theropoda
Family: Neovenatoridae

• The only known specimens of *Fukuiraptor* are quite small and may be juveniles. The adults may be much larger.

FUKUISAURUS

foo-KOO-ee-SAW-rus

PLANT-EATER

EARLY CRETACEOUS

DANGER LEVEL 2

Place to spot: Japan
Habitat: Forests and plains
When: 128 mya
Name means: Fukui lizard
Alert: Large and clumsy

GENTLE GIANT

The *Fukuisaurus* is an ornithopod, one of the most common types of dinosaur in the Early Cretaceous period. Though up to nearly 16 feet long and weighing some 90 pounds, it's a gentle giant that feeds only on plants.

USEFUL TIP!

Keep your distance, as these dinosaurs are probably preyed upon by *Fukuiraptor*.

Strong back

Jaws have limited mobility

Stocky tail

Legs provide strong base

Splayed feet for balance

Hands used for both grasping and walking

NO WAY!

The dinosaur's jaw is not very mobile. In fact, it cannot move its jaws sideways to chew.

FOUR OR TWO

The *Fukuisaurus* can stand on either four or two legs. This allows it to reach up and graze the vegetation at the tops of high plants.

Length: 15 ft.
Diet: Plants
Group: Ornithopoda
Family: Hadrosauridae

• *Fukuisaurus* is known from just a few pieces of skull. However, scientists believe that its body looks very similar to that of *Iguanodon*.

Place to spot: Argentina
Habitat: Tropical plains
When: 87 mya
Name means: Giant chief lizard
Alert: Massive size

NO WAY!

Futalognkosaurus has an enormous neck with 14 huge vertebrae.

Small head

LAST OF THE TITANS

Futalognkosaurus is a titanosaur, the last great group of sauropods. It has a wide, thick body that counterbalances its long neck, which it holds up high to feed on tall trees.

Thick, heavy neck

USEFUL TIP!

It may be slow, but beware of this animal's whiplike tail.

FAMILY MEAL

Adults probably pull down branches for younger dinosaurs that are too short to reach them. When the young grow to about one year old, they feed on bushes. Adults can grow up to 80 feet.

Extremely bulky hips

Pillarlike legs

Whiplike tail

FUTALOGNKOSAURUS

FOO-ta-logn-koh-SAW-rus

PLANT-EATER

LATE CRETACEOUS

DANGER LEVEL 3

Fleshy pads under feet

Length: 80 ft.
Diet: Plants
Group: Sauropodomorpha
Family: Titanosauridae

• About 70 percent of *Futalognkosaurus'* skeleton has been found, making it the most complete of the giant dinosaurs.

GALLIMIMUS

GAL-ee-MY-mus

OMNIVORE

LATE CRETACEOUS

DANGER LEVEL 3

Place to spot: Mongolia
Habitat: River valleys
When: 74–70 mya
Name means: Chicken mimic
Alert: Very fast runner

AGILE RUNNER

Gallimimus runs clear of an *Albertosaurus* at speeds of 30 mph. It can change direction quickly, dodging and weaving out of reach.

NO WAY!

Gallimimus has large eyes, maybe for hunting at night. It has a wide range of vision but not good depth perception.

Birdlike skull

Toothless beak

Slender, flexible neck

FAST MOVER

This theropod stands about twice as high as an adult human. It is one of the fastest dinosaurs and can outrun a tyrannosaur. *Gallimimus'* arms are long enough to reach the ground to grab plants, lizards, and other small prey.

Long arms

Long, powerful legs

BEAK

Gallimimus has a sharp, narrow beak. This is perfect for catching such food as insects, small animals, or eggs that it can swallow in one gulp.

USEFUL TIP!

Don't get in this animal's way when it's running at full speed!

Length: 20 ft.
Diet: Plants, insects
Group: Theropoda
Family: Ornithomimidae

• At more than 10 feet tall and 20 feet long, *Gallimimus* is one of the largest of the ornithomimids.

Place to spot: USA
Habitat: Woodland
When: 154–142 mya
Name means: Gargoyle lizard
Alert: Dangerous tail

HEAVY ARMOR

This is one of the earliest ankylosaurs and one of only two, so far, from the Jurassic. It has a thick plate over its pelvis with short spikes on the back and longer spines along the sides. This armor looks similar to that of a modern lizard, such as the moloch, or thorny devil.

NO WAY!

Gargoyleosaurus eats low-lying plants, such as ferns, and weighs up to a ton.

USEFUL TIP!

Gargoyleosaurus can be spotted munching on ferns.

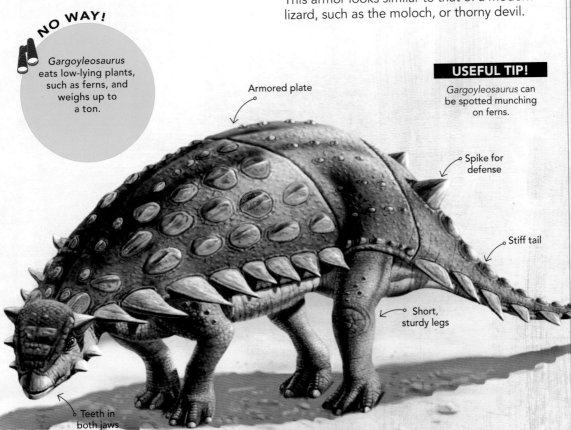

Armored plate

Spike for defense

Stiff tail

Short, sturdy legs

Teeth in both jaws

SPIKES AND TEETH

A set of sideways-facing spikes runs along each side of its body. Unusually, the front part of its mouth has seven teeth—most ankylosaurs have no teeth in the front of their beaklike mouth.

GARGOYLEOSAURUS

gar-GOYL-ee-o-SAW-rus

PLANT-EATER

LATE JURASSIC

DANGER LEVEL 3

Length: 10–13 ft.
Diet: Plants
Group: Ankylosauria
Family: Nodosauridae

• *Gargoyleosaurus* is known from a partially complete fossil skeleton discovered in 1996, and two other partial skeletons.

SPIKES AND SHIELDS

Gastonia has a shield over its pelvis and large, pointed spikes on its back. Small, sideways-facing spikes go all the way down its tail. It uses its armor to fight off predators, such as *Utahraptor*, which lives in the same area.

Place to spot: USA
Habitat: Forest
When: 125 mya
Name means: For (Robert) Gaston
Alert: Covered in sharp spikes

USEFUL TIP!

Stay away from the very large and sharp shoulder spikes.

NO WAY!

To eat them, predators have to flip ankylosaurs over, exposing their soft bellies.

Small spikes on top of tail

Pelvic shield

Sideways-pointing spikes

Large shoulder spikes

NO CLUBBING

Gastonia is one of the most heavily armored ankylosaurs—but, unlike some other species, it does not have a tail club.

GASTONIA
gas-TOH-nee-a

PLANT-EATER

EARLY CRETACEOUS

DANGER LEVEL 3

Stubby feet

Eats low-lying plants

Length: 16 ft.
Diet: Plants
Group: Ankylosauria
Family: Nodosauridae

• *Gastonia* was discovered in the same quarry as the fearsome *Utahraptor*, which was probably one of its main predators.

Place to spot: USA
Habitat: Open woodland
When: 139–134 mya
Name means: Twin seizer
Alert: Sharp teeth

GEMINIRAPTOR
JEM-i-nee-RAP-tor

MEAT-EATER

EARLY CRETACEOUS

DANGER LEVEL 2

USEFUL TIP!

Despite its size, this dinosaur can still give a nasty bite.

FEATHERS

Birdlike feathers coat the arms and tail of *Geminiraptor*, while its body is covered in downy feathers. This helps the dinosaur control its temperature when it is attacking its prey.

Feathers cover the body and limbs

38 teeth in its upper jaw

Long tail feathers help with balance when chasing prey

Short thighbone suggests it is a fast runner

INSECT-EATER

Geminiraptor has small teeth and may live on a diet of insects and very small animals. Although it is not very big, it is still bigger than other Early Cretaceous troodontids, such as *Sinovenator*, which helps tell these dinosaurs apart.

NO WAY!

The site *Geminiraptor* came from was found by identical twin geologists Drs. Celina and Marina Suarez—*gemini* means "twins" in Latin.

Large second toe for holding and tearing prey

Length: 5 ft.
Diet: Meat
Group: Theropoda
Family: Troodontidae

• *Geminiraptor* is the first troodont dinosaur known to have lived in Early Cretaceous North America.

GIGANOTOSAURUS

jig-an-OH-toe-SAW-rus

MEAT-EATER

MID-CRETACEOUS

DANGER LEVEL 5

Place to spot: Argentina
Habitat: Floodplain
When: 112–90 mya
Name means: Giant southern lizard
Alert: Powerful hunter

NO WAY!

Giganotosaurus lived alongside some of the biggest-ever sauropods, but was large enough to prey on them.

MASSIVE MEAT-EATER

Giganotosaurus is one of the largest theropods ever to walk the Earth. Its skull alone is almost 6 feet long. There is strong competition for the title of "largest predatory dinosaur of all time" between this dinosaur and a number of other theropods.

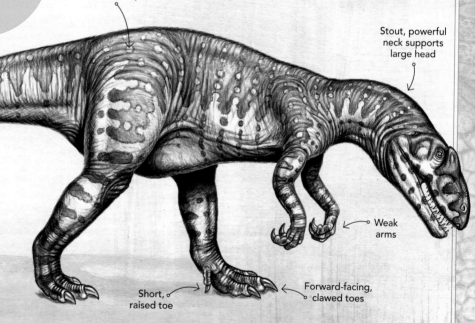

Center of gravity is in the hips

Stout, powerful neck supports large head

Long, heavy tail

Weak arms

Short, raised toe

Forward-facing, clawed toes

PACK HUNTER

Several *Giganotosaurus* skeletons have been found close together, which suggests they move and hunt in groups, and use pack-hunting techniques to catch their prey.

USEFUL TIP!

Don't stand downwind. *Giganotosaurus* has a very good sense of smell!

Length: Up to 43 ft.
Diet: Meat
Group: Theropoda
Family: Carcharodontosauridae

• *Giganotosaurus* is so large that it probably cannot run faster than 30 mph without losing its balance.

Place to spot: China
Habitat: Arid plains
When: 80–70 mya
Name means: Giant thief
Alert: High-speed hunter

BIG BIRD

This giant, birdlike dinosaur is 16 feet tall and weighs 2 tons. From studies of its known remains, scientists know that it is not yet fully grown. It has a toothless beak and claws. Although no feathers have been found with the bones, they are common in this kind of dinosaur.

NO WAY!

Gigantoraptor's circular nests are 10 feet wide and have a space in the middle for the adult to sit without damaging the eggs.

USEFUL TIP!

This dinosaur scares easily and runs. Stay clear!

Birdlike hip bones

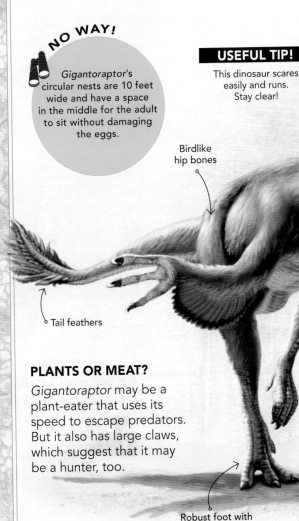

Toothless beak

Tail feathers

Arms possibly feathered

PLANTS OR MEAT?

Gigantoraptor may be a plant-eater that uses its speed to escape predators. But it also has large claws, which suggest that it may be a hunter, too.

Robust foot with strongly curved toe claws

GIGANTORAPTOR
gee-GAN-toe-RAP-tor

OMNIVORE

LATE CRETACEOUS

DANGER LEVEL 3

Length: 26 ft.
Diet: Possibly plants
Group: Theropoda
Family: Oviraptoridae

• *Gigantoraptor* lays enormous eggs that are up to 20 inches long. In the nests, they are arranged in large rings 10 feet wide.

GUANLONG
GWAN-long

MEAT-EATER

LATE JURASSIC

DANGER LEVEL 4

Place to spot: China
Habitat: Forest
When: 159–154 mya
Name means: Crowned dragon
Alert: Hunts in packs

Arched back

Feathers

Hollow crest

USEFUL TIP!
Its crest is probably brightly colored, making it easy to spot.

Overhanging teeth

FORERUNNER

Living in the Late Jurassic period, *Guanlong* is one of the earliest tyrannosaurs. It has a 2½-inch-high crest on the top of its head. The crest is too delicate to be used in combat. Instead, it is probably used only to attract a mate or to identify itself as a *Guanlong*.

NO WAY!

Later tyrannosaurs have two fingers on each hand, but *Guanlong* has three.

Three long fingers

Powerful hind claws

LITTLE REX

This dinosaur is about 4 feet tall at the hips—about a third of the size of its relative *Tyrannosaurus rex*.

Length: 10 ft.
Diet: Meat
Group: Theropoda
Family: Undecided

• The first *Guanlong* specimens, an adult and a juvenile, were stumbled upon by accident by a laborer in northwest China.

Place to spot: Argentina
Habitat: Forests and floodplains
When: 235–230 mya
Name means: Herrera's lizard
Alert: Fast runner

HERRERASAURUS
heh-RARE-uh-SAW-rus

MEAT-EATER

MID-TRIASSIC

DANGER LEVEL 3

MYSTERY CREATURE

According to some scientists, *Herrerasaurus* is an archosaur, a crocodile ancestor that is common in Triassic times. However, it is now thought to be a theropodlike early dinosaur.

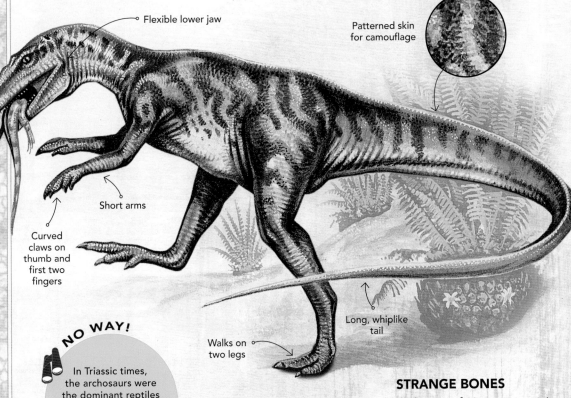

Flexible lower jaw

Patterned skin for camouflage

Short arms

Curved claws on thumb and first two fingers

Long, whiplike tail

Walks on two legs

NO WAY!

In Triassic times, the archosaurs were the dominant reptiles and had the edge over dinosaurs, but not for long.

USEFUL TIP!

Watch out for this dinosaur's large, canine teeth.

STRANGE BONES

Only two of *Herrerasaurus'* vertebrae are attached to its hip bone. Other dinosaurs have three vertebrae attached to theirs.

Length: 10–13 ft.
Diet: Meat
Group: Theropoda
Family: Herrerasauridae

• Though the first fossils of *Herrerasaurus* were found in 1958, little was known about the animal until an almost complete skeleton was found in 1988.

HETERODONTOSAURUS
HET-uh-roh-DONT-o-SAW-rus

OMNIVORE

EARLY JURASSIC

DANGER LEVEL 2

Place to spot: South Africa
Habitat: Near lakes
When: 208–200 mya
Name means: Differently toothed lizard
Alert: Long, sharp fangs

USEFUL TIP!

It may look fierce, but this dinosaur eats only plants and small insects.

MANY KINDS OF TEETH

Normally, the teeth in a dinosaur's mouth all look the same, but this dinosaur has three kinds of teeth. Its front ones are designed to clip plants. Right behind these is a set of fangs. It also has cheek teeth for chomping foliage.

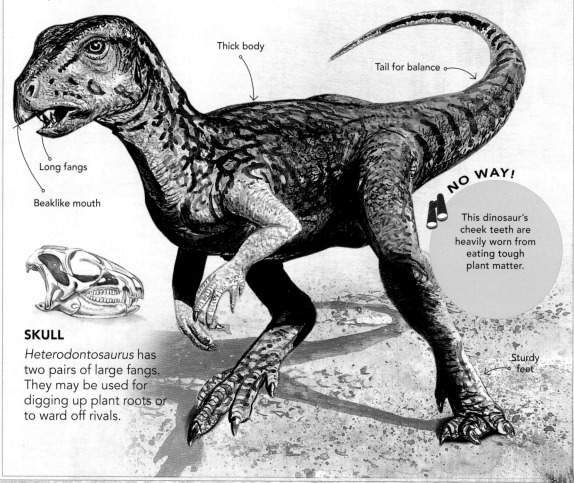

Thick body

Tail for balance

Long fangs

Beaklike mouth

NO WAY!

This dinosaur's cheek teeth are heavily worn from eating tough plant matter.

Sturdy feet

SKULL

Heterodontosaurus has two pairs of large fangs. They may be used for digging up plant roots or to ward off rivals.

Length: 4 ft.
Diet: Plants, small animals
Group: Cerapoda
Family: Heterodontosauridae

• *Heterodontosaurus* has five fingers on each hand. Two of these fingers oppose each other, allowing the dinosaur to pick things up.

Place to spot: USA
Habitat: Scrub and conifer woodland
When: 124 mya
Name means: Horse dragon
Alert: Strong, biting beak

NO WAY!

The bones of *Hippodraco* were found with those of other dinosaurs, a crocodile, and a mammal skull.

USEFUL TIP!

Look for *Hippodraco* living in herds with other iguanodontids for protection.

HORSE HEAD

Hippodraco's teeth are shield-shaped, like most iguanodontids', and it has a long skull scientists think looks a bit like the shape of a horse's. This is why this dinosaur is named *Hippodraco*—hippo means "horse" in Greek.

Shield-shaped teeth

Long tail

Powerful beak

Huge thumb claw

CAREFUL EATER

This medium-sized iguanodontid probably walks on two legs and feeds on all fours. It can be seen eating plants quite low to the ground while keeping a lookout for predatory theropods searching for a quick snack.

HIPPODRACO

hip-o-DRAH-co

PLANT-EATER

EARLY CRETACEOUS

DANGER LEVEL 2

Length: 15 ft.
Diet: Plants
Group: Ornithopoda
Family: Undecided

• The eye socket of *Hippodraco* is large, and scientists think this means it is from a younger individual rather than an adult.

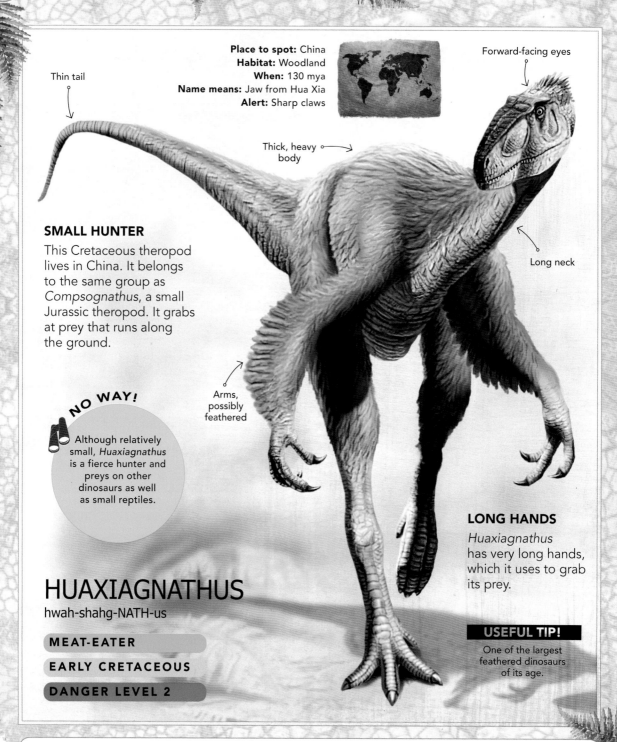

Thin tail

Place to spot: China
Habitat: Woodland
When: 130 mya
Name means: Jaw from Hua Xia
Alert: Sharp claws

Forward-facing eyes

Thick, heavy body

Long neck

SMALL HUNTER

This Cretaceous theropod lives in China. It belongs to the same group as *Compsognathus*, a small Jurassic theropod. It grabs at prey that runs along the ground.

Arms, possibly feathered

NO WAY!

Although relatively small, *Huaxiagnathus* is a fierce hunter and preys on other dinosaurs as well as small reptiles.

LONG HANDS

Huaxiagnathus has very long hands, which it uses to grab its prey.

HUAXIAGNATHUS

hwah-shahg-NATH-us

MEAT-EATER

EARLY CRETACEOUS

DANGER LEVEL 2

USEFUL TIP!

One of the largest feathered dinosaurs of its age.

Length: 6 ft.
Diet: Meat
Group: Theropoda
Family: Compsognathidae

• *Hauxiagnathus* is named after the old name for China, Hua Xia. It is known from two skeletons found in the Yixian Formation.

Places to spot: England, Spain
Habitat: Open woodland
When: 125–120 mya
Name means: High-crested tooth
Alert: Very fast runner

HYPSILOPHODON
hip-seh-LOF-o-don

PLANT-EATER

EARLY CRETACEOUS

DANGER LEVEL 1

Large eyes

Long, stiff tail

Camouflage

Teeth are constantly replaced as they wear out

Plates of internal armor between ribs

Five fingers

Long legs

SWIFT RUNNER

This small plant-eater lives in the Early Cretaceous. It has features of dinosaurs from millions of years earlier, with five fingers on each hand and teeth rather than a beak. It has a lightweight skeleton, low posture, long legs, and a stiff tail. This means that it is a very fast runner.

Place to spot: USA
Habitat: Scrub and conifer woodland
When: 124 mya
Name means: Colossal iguana
Alert: Large with a powerful beak

IGUANACOLOSSUS
ig-WAHN-ah-coh-LOS-us

PLANT-EATER

EARLY CRETACEOUS

DANGER LEVEL 2

Dense, heavy body

USEFUL TIP!
Look for *Iguanacolossus* on two or four legs and living in herds.

Chunky limbs

PRIMITIVE BEAST

This large, 5.5 ton iguanodontid is about the same size as *Iguanodon*, which lives in Europe. *Iguanacolossus* has a long, narrow skull with a beak for snipping off leaves. Its mouth is packed with teeth for chewing up plants.

Length: 6–7 ft.
Diet: Plants
Group: Clypeodonta
Family: Hypsilophodontidae

Length: 30 ft.
Diet: Plants
Group: Ornithopoda
Family: Undecided

ANATOMY

Iguanodon has strong hind legs with three hoofed toes. It spends some time on all fours but runs on its hind legs.

Places to spot: England, Belgium, Germany, France, Spain
Habitat: Woodland
When: 125 mya
Name means: Iguana tooth
Alert: Lethal thumb spike

NO WAY!

Iguanodon has a great sense of smell, and can sniff out its favorite plants from far away.

THUMB SPIKE

This is one of the best-known dinosaurs. Its most famous feature is its thumb spike, which will take out the eye of any theropod that gets too near. It uses its horny beak to graze on tough plants. It chews its food with rows of ridged teeth to grind it into a pulp.

FLEXIBLE HAND

Iguanodon uses its 8-inch-long thumb spike as a dagger. The fifth finger can bend and grasp plants and other objects.

Striped skin for camouflage

Tough beak

Stiff tail

Three-toed back legs

Thumb spike

IGUANODON

ig-WAHN-o-don

PLANT-EATER

EARLY CRETACEOUS

DANGER LEVEL 2

USEFUL TIP!

Iguanodon lives in herds to protect it from predators.

Length: 33 ft.
Diet: Plants
Group: Ornithopoda
Family: Iguanodontidae

• *Iguanodon* was one of the first dinosaurs to be reconstructed, in 1852 in London. In 1878, miners in Belgium found a layer of rock with 38 *Iguanodon* skeletons.

Place to spot: China
Habitat: Forest
When: 130–125 mya
Name means: Incisor lizard
Alert: May be an omnivore

TAIL DISPLAY

Like a peacock, *Incisivosaurus* may be able to spread out its tail feathers into a fan to make a display to attract mates.

Large eye

POSSIBLE OMNIVORE

This tiny birdlike theropod belongs to the same group as *Oviraptor*, but it is an earlier dinosaur. It has ratlike front teeth instead of the toothless beak of its relatives—perhaps it is on the way to becoming a plant-eater.

Shorter feathers on body

Small back teeth

Feathers on arm for display

Longer feathers on tail

Claws on feet

NO WAY!

Incisivosaurus has heavy bones. Even with larger wings, it would struggle to fly.

ODD ONE OUT

Most *Oviraptors* have no teeth, but *Incisivosaurus* has enlarged "canines" up front plus peglike teeth in its cheek area. Some scientists think this dinosaur is the same dinosaur as *Protarchaeopteryx*.

INCISIVOSAURUS
in-sai-see-vo-SAW-rus

OMNIVORE

EARLY CRETACEOUS

DANGER LEVEL 1

USEFUL TIP!

Incisivosaurus is about the same size as a large bird.

Length: 3 ft.
Diet: Plants, small animals
Group: Theropoda
Family: Undecided

• The *Incisivosaurus* fossil remains include a 4-inch-long skull with almost perfectly preserved teeth, which give us clues as to what the dinosaur eats.

JINGSHANOSAURUS

JING-SHAHN-o-SAW-us

PLANT-EATER

EARLY JURASSIC

DANGER LEVEL 2

Place to spot: China
Habitat: Forests and plains
When: 205–190 mya
Name means: Lizard from Jingshan
Alert: Powerful claws

WOOD-EATER

Jingshanosaurus is one of the last prosauropods, and unlike later sauropods is bipedal. It has powerful back legs and a strong tail as a counterbalance to the body and long neck. Its skull is full of teeth that it uses to eat thick, woody plant material.

USEFUL TIP!

Closely related to *Yunnanosaurus.*

NO WAY!

Weighing up to 2 tons, *Jingshanosaurus* is one of the largest dinosaurs of its day.

Small head

Long neck

Short forearms

Clawed thumb

Long tail

Long legs

THUMB CLAW

The thumb has a large claw, which the dinosaur uses for defense.

Length: 28 ft.
Diet: Plants
Group: Sauropodomorpha
Family: Plateosauria

• Scientists have found a nearly complete skeleton. A cast of the skeleton toured the world in the late 1990s.

Place to spot: Germany
Habitat: Near lakes
When: 154–151 mya
Name means: Jura hunter
Alert: Nocturnal

JURAVENATOR
JOO-rah-ven-AY-tor

MEAT-EATER

LATE JURASSIC

DANGER LEVEL 1

ANCESTOR OF BIRDS

This tiny theropod is an example of a coelurosaur, an ancestor of modern birds. The fossil found is that of a young dinosaur, which fell on its back into a lake. It has a scaly tail, but other parts of its body may be covered in downy feathers.

USEFUL TIP!

This tiny predator will be more scared of you than you are of it.

Downy feathers

Scaly tail

Serrated teeth

Feathers on arms

Long claws

NO WAY!

It took 700 hours for scientists to scrape away the limestone surrounding the fossil of this dinosaur.

NIGHT HUNTER

Juravenator's big eyes show that it probably comes out at night, when larger predators are not around.

Length: 28–32 in.
Diet: Meat
Group: Theropoda
Family: Compsognathidae

• A patch of skin, found with the bones, shows that *Juravenator* has scales. There are also traces of what may be simple feathers.

KENTROSAURUS
KEN-TRO-SAW-rus

PLANT-EATER

LATE JURASSIC

DANGER LEVEL 3

Place to spot: Tanzania
Habitat: Forests and plains
When: 155–140 mya
Name means: Spike lizard
Alert: Tail is a dangerous weapon

NO WAY!

Much of the original fossils of *Kentrosaurus* were kept in a German museum. They were destroyed by bombing during World War II.

Plates

PLATED STEGOSAUR

This Jurassic dinosaur is closely related to the American *Stegosaurus*, but it lives in Tanzania, Africa. It has pairs of plates along its neck and back, and pairs of small spikes along its hips and tail.

Sharp spikes

Strong, flexible tail

Back legs bear most of its weight

Small head contains walnut-sized brain

USEFUL TIP!

This dinosaur is slow moving, but keep clear of that tail!

DEFENSIVE TAIL

When threatened, *Kentrosaurus* will spin around on its hind legs to point its tail at its enemy.

Length: Up to 16 ft.
Diet: Plants
Group: Stegosauria
Family: Stegosauridae

• The dinosaur's plates and spikes were found away from the rest of the skeleton, so we do not know for sure where they were on the body.

Place to spot: Russia
Habitat: Forests
When: 65 mya
Name means: Kerberos lizard
Alert: Slow moving

KERBEROSAURUS
ker-BAIR-oh-SAW-rus

> **PLANT-EATER**
> **LATE CRETACEOUS**
> **DANGER LEVEL 2**

DUCK BILL

This duck-billed dinosaur lives in Asia toward the end of the Mesozoic era. Its ancestors walked to Asia from North America about 10 million years earlier.

Small, flat head

Spine

Tough palate

NO WAY!

Kerberosaurus is closely related to *Prosaurolophus* from North America, but the two dinosaurs evolved in different ways.

Stiff tail

CHEWING PLANTS

Kerberosaurus has lots of teeth, and its upper jaw is hinged with the skull to allow it to chew tough food more easily.

Clawed toes

Strong front legs

USEFUL TIP!

Kerberosaurus can walk on two legs or on all fours.

Length: 30 ft.
Diet: Plants
Group: Ornithopoda
Family: Hadrosauridae

- *Kerberosaurus* remains were found in the Amur region of eastern Russia alongside the fossils of hollow-crested hadrosaurs.

KOSMOCERATOPS
KOZ-mo-SER-a-tops

PLANT-EATER

LATE CRETACEOUS

DANGER LEVEL 3

Place to spot: USA
Habitat: Damp alluvial plain
When: 76 mya
Name means: Ornate horned face
Alert: Outward-pointing horns

NO WAY!

Kosmoceratops has the most elaborate skull of any ceratopsian.

USEFUL TIP!

Kosmoceratops can be spotted living in herds.

SHORT FRILL

Kosmoceratops' frill is part of a 6-foot-long skull. This is nearly half the length of the whole dinosaur.

Short, wide frill

Long, outward-pointing spikes

Short cheek horns

FEARSOME DEFENSES

Kosmoceratops has more horns than any other dinosaur. It has ten hooklike spikes on the back of its frill, two brow horns that point up and outward, a bit like a bison's, a blunt horn on its nose, and small horns that jut out from its cheeks.

Length: 15 ft.
Diet: Plants
Group: Ceratopsia
Family: Ceratopsidae

• The spiky skulls may be used more as a way to find a mate than as a defense against predators.

Place to spot: Canada/USA
Habitat: Forest
When: 76–74 mya
Name means: Lambe's lizard
Alert: Mostly peaceful herbivore

USEFUL TIP!

The size of the crest will tell you how old the dinosaur is.

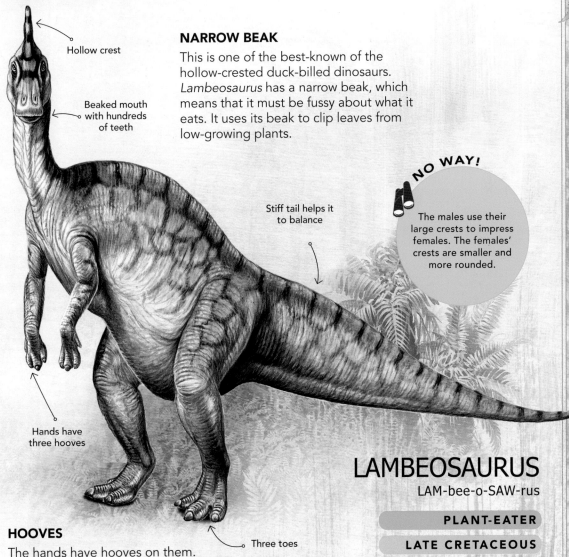

Hollow crest

Beaked mouth with hundreds of teeth

NARROW BEAK

This is one of the best-known of the hollow-crested duck-billed dinosaurs. *Lambeosaurus* has a narrow beak, which means that it must be fussy about what it eats. It uses its beak to clip leaves from low-growing plants.

NO WAY!

The males use their large crests to impress females. The females' crests are smaller and more rounded.

Stiff tail helps it to balance

Hands have three hooves

Three toes

HOOVES

The hands have hooves on them. This shows that *Lambeosaurus* can walk on all fours.

LAMBEOSAURUS
LAM-bee-o-SAW-rus

PLANT-EATER

LATE CRETACEOUS

DANGER LEVEL 2

Length: 54 ft.
Diet: Leaves and fruit
Group: Ornithopoda
Family: Hadrosauridae

• *Lambeosaurus* was discovered by Lawrence Lambe in 1902, but it was not identified as a separate genus until more than 20 years later.

LEAELLYNASAURA

lee-ELL-in-a-SAW-ruh

PLANT-EATER

EARLY CRETACEOUS

DANGER LEVEL 1

Place to spot: Australia
Habitat: Antarctic forest
When: 115–110 mya
Name means: Leaellyn's lizard
Alert: Fast runner

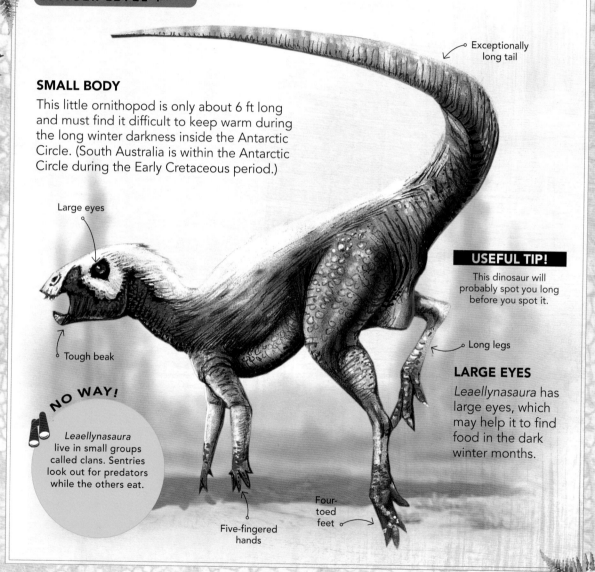

○ Exceptionally long tail

SMALL BODY

This little ornithopod is only about 6 ft long and must find it difficult to keep warm during the long winter darkness inside the Antarctic Circle. (South Australia is within the Antarctic Circle during the Early Cretaceous period.)

Large eyes ○

○ Tough beak

NO WAY!

Leaellynasaura live in small groups called clans. Sentries look out for predators while the others eat.

Five-fingered hands

Four-toed feet ○

USEFUL TIP!

This dinosaur will probably spot you long before you spot it.

○ Long legs

LARGE EYES

Leaellynasaura has large eyes, which may help it to find food in the dark winter months.

Length: 6 ft.
Diet: Plants
Group: Ornithopoda
Family: Undecided

• We know about *Leaellynasaura* from the skull fragments and bones of a juvenile discovered in Australia's Dinosaur Cove in 1989.

Place to spot: China
Habitat: Forest
When: 125–113 mya
Name means: Lizard from Liaoning
Alert: Ventral plating

ARMORED UNDERSIDE

This dinosaur is a baby. Unlike any other ankylosaur, *Liaoningosaurus* has armor on its belly—known as ventral plating—not just on its back and sides.

NO WAY!

This dinosaur shows a confusing mix of nodosaurid and ankylosaurid features, so we don't quite know how to classify it.

As it gets older, spikes will grow from the shoulder

USEFUL TIP!

The adults will be much bigger than this juvenile, so watch out!

Strong tail

Large skull

Long teeth

Ventral plating

Sharp claws

UNKNOWN ADULT

We don't know what the adult *Liaoningosaurus* looks like. It may not have ventral plating, because it may be so big and fierce that it does not need it.

LIAONINGOSAURUS
LE-OH-ning-o-SAW-rus

PLANT-EATER

EARLY CRETACEOUS

DANGER LEVEL 1

Length: 6–10 ft. (adult)
Diet: Plants
Group: Ankylosauria
Family: Ankylosauridae

• Only one fossil of *Liaoningosaurus* has been found, but it is a complete skeleton. It was found in the Yixian Formation in China.

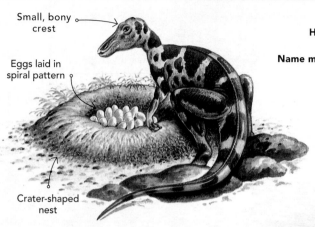

Small, bony crest

Eggs laid in spiral pattern

Crater-shaped nest

Place to spot: USA
Habitat: Forests and plains
When: 80–74 mya
Name means: Good mother lizard
Alert: Protective mothers will be fierce

GOOD MOTHERS

Maiasaura take good care of their young and are known as nurturers. Females nest in large groups.

GROWTH SPURT

Baby *Maiasaura* grow very quickly. They are already 4 feet long by the end of their first year, and their parents are kept busy feeding them. However, they still have a long way to grow before they reach their full adult size of 30 feet or more.

NO WAY!

It is possible that all hadrosaurs nest in this way, forming vast nesting colonies, as seabirds do today.

Rodlike bones stick up from back

Narrow tail

Narrow bill

MAIASAURA

MY-ah-SAW-ruh

PLANT-EATER

LATE CRETACEOUS

DANGER LEVEL 2

USEFUL TIP!

Only the adults have the small, bony crest in front of their eyes.

Length: 30 ft.
Diet: Plants
Group: Ornithopoda
Family: Hadrosauridae

• Many fossilzed *Maiasaura* nests with egg fragments and some babies have been found in Montana. This has allowed scientists to build a detailed picture of its life cycle.

Place to spot: Madagascar
Habitat: Coastal plains
When: 70–65 mya
Name means: Lizard from Mahajanga
Alert: Powerful jaws

MAJUNGASAURUS
mah-JOONG-ah-SAW-rus

MEAT-EATER

LATE CRETACEOUS

DANGER LEVEL 5

Horn on head used for display

NO WAY!

Majungasaurus fight each other over food. Sometimes they will kill their opponents and eat them as well.

HUNTER AND SCAVENGER

This theropod is both a predator and a scavenger. Its favorite prey includes sauropods, such as *Rapetosaurus*. It kills with a single bite to the neck, holding on until its prey stops struggling, as cats do today.

Tough, armor-plated skin

Stiff tail

Thick neck

Finger bones are fused together

Stocky legs

Clawed toes

STRONG TEETH

The front teeth of the upper jaw are particularly strong so that they do not break when holding on to struggling prey.

USEFUL TIP!

Can be spotted on tidal flats searching for carcasses.

Length: 20-23 ft.
Diet: Meat
Group: Theropoda
Family: Abelisauridae

• *Majungasaurus* is known from many fossils, including a complete skull. One of the skeletons has had its tail bitten off.

MAMENCHISAURUS

mah-MUN-kee-SAW-rus

PLANT-EATER

LATE JURASSIC

DANGER LEVEL 4

Place to spot: China
Habitat: Woodland
When: 160–145 mya
Name means: Lizard from Mamenchi (China)
Alert: Dangerous tail

NO WAY!

The largest *Mamenchisaurus* specimen has a 43-foot-long neck—that's longer than seven adult humans lying head to toe!

Tiny head

LONG NECK

This giant sauropod has one of the longest necks of any known animal. Hollow chambers on each side of the neck bones make the neck lighter. It is counterbalanced by the heavy body and long tail.

Enormous neck

Long front legs

Very long tail

Broad feet

USEFUL TIP!

Uses its long neck to feed on soft leaves at the tops of trees.

BIG BONES

Mamenchisaurus' neck contains 19 bones—more than any other dinosaur. The neck bones are twice as long as the bones in its back.

Length: Up to 82 ft.
Diet: Plants
Group: Sauropodomorpha
Family: Eusauropoda

• *Mamenchisaurus* remains include some of the most complete sauropod skeletons known. One specimen has a fully intact neck.

Place to spot: Madagascar
Habitat: Woodland
When: 70 mya
Name means: Vicious lizard
Alert: Small but aggressive

NO WAY!

Masiakasaurus catches small fish by thrusting its head into the water and using its sharp front teeth as spears.

STRANGE JAW

Masiakasaurus has a unique jaw and tooth structure. The tips of both jaws curve outward, making it look as if its teeth point forward. These small teeth are adapted for grabbing, not for ripping or tearing.

Straight neck

USEFUL TIP!

May be found near water hunting fish.

Slim tail

Long arms

Long claws on fingers

Masiakasaurus has caught a small snake

Walks on three toes

MASIAKASAURUS
mah-SHEE-ah-kah-SAW-rus

MEAT-EATER

LATE CRETACEOUS

DANGER LEVEL 2

SMALL DINOSAUR

This small predator has to watch out for larger predators that will prey on it, including the fearsome *Majungasaurus*.

Length: Up to 6 ft.
Diet: Meat
Group: Theropoda
Family: Noasauridae

• Forward-facing teeth are found in several groups of flying and swimming reptiles and are well adapted to catching fish.

MASSOSPONDYLUS
mass-o-SPON-die-lus

OMNIVORE

EARLY JURASSIC

DANGER LEVEL 3

Places to spot: South Africa, Lesotho, Zimbabwe
Habitat: Woodlands
When: 208–183 mya
Name means: Elongated vertebra
Alert: Large front claws

RESTING ON ALL FOURS

This dinosaur's back legs are much longer than its front ones. It might rest on all four legs but moves around on two legs, as its hands have large claws that make walking on them impossible. *Massospondylus* eats mostly plants, but will also occasionally feast on small animals.

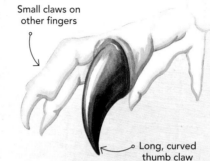

Small claws on other fingers

Long, curved thumb claw

THUMB CLAWS

Massospondylus has a large, sicklelike thumb claw on each hand. These are used to ward off predators.

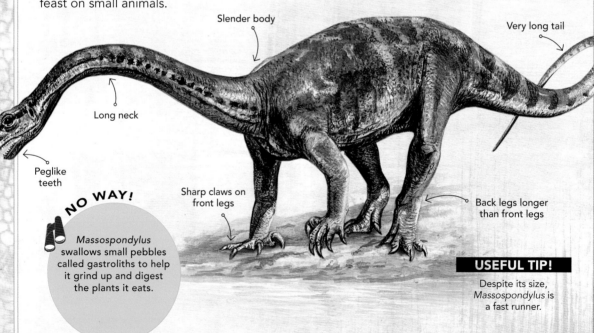

Slender body

Very long tail

Long neck

Peglike teeth

NO WAY!

Massospondylus swallows small pebbles called gastroliths to help it grind up and digest the plants it eats.

Sharp claws on front legs

Back legs longer than front legs

USEFUL TIP!

Despite its size, *Massospondylus* is a fast runner.

Length: 13 ft.
Diet: Plants and meat
Group: Sauropodomorpha
Family: Massospondylidae

• *Massospondylus* was discovered in the nineteenth century. Since then, more than 80 incomplete skeletons have been found, as well as six eggs.

Place to spot: England
Habitat: Forests
When: 176–161 mya
Name means: Great lizard
Alert: Fast runner

USEFUL TIP!

It has a small, bony ridge over each eye.

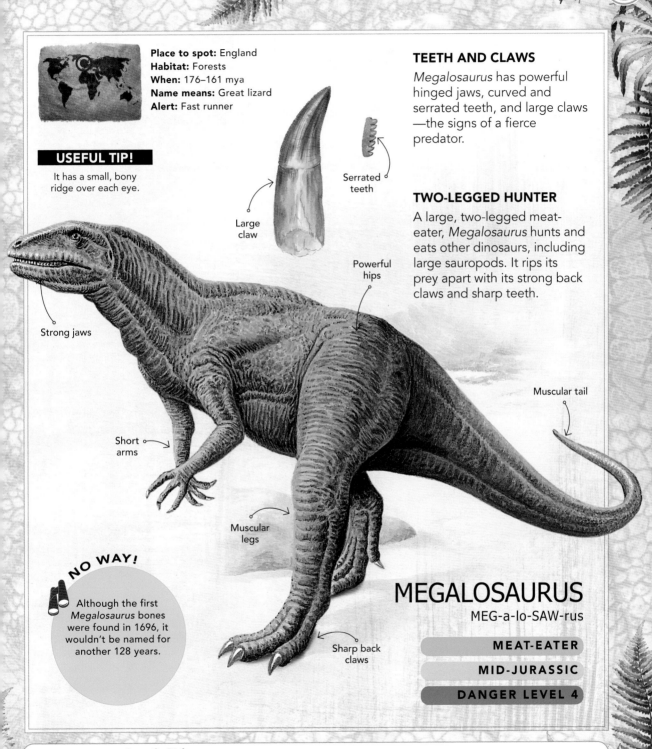

Large claw

Serrated teeth

Strong jaws

Short arms

Powerful hips

Muscular tail

Muscular legs

NO WAY!

Although the first *Megalosaurus* bones were found in 1696, it wouldn't be named for another 128 years.

TEETH AND CLAWS

Megalosaurus has powerful hinged jaws, curved and serrated teeth, and large claws —the signs of a fierce predator.

TWO-LEGGED HUNTER

A large, two-legged meat-eater, *Megalosaurus* hunts and eats other dinosaurs, including large sauropods. It rips its prey apart with its strong back claws and sharp teeth.

MEGALOSAURUS
MEG-a-lo-SAW-rus

Sharp back claws

MEAT-EATER

MID-JURASSIC

DANGER LEVEL 4

Length: 30 ft.
Diet: Meat
Group: Theropoda
Family: Megalosauridae

• *Megalosaurus* was the first dinosaur to be discovered and the first to be given a scientific name, by English palaeontologist William Buckland in 1824.

LONG SLEEP

If only all dinosaur discoveries were as spectacular as this one! This animal was found in a sleeping position with its head tucked under its forearm—a pose typical of resting birds today. It probably suffocated quickly from poisonous volcanic gases.

Place to spot: China
Habitat: Woodland
When: 140–135 mya
Name means: Sleeping soundly
Alert: Very small

NO WAY!

This dinosaur's species name, *Mei long,* is Chinese for "sleeping soundly like a dragon."

USEFUL TIP!

Look out for *Mei* on wooded volcanic slopes.

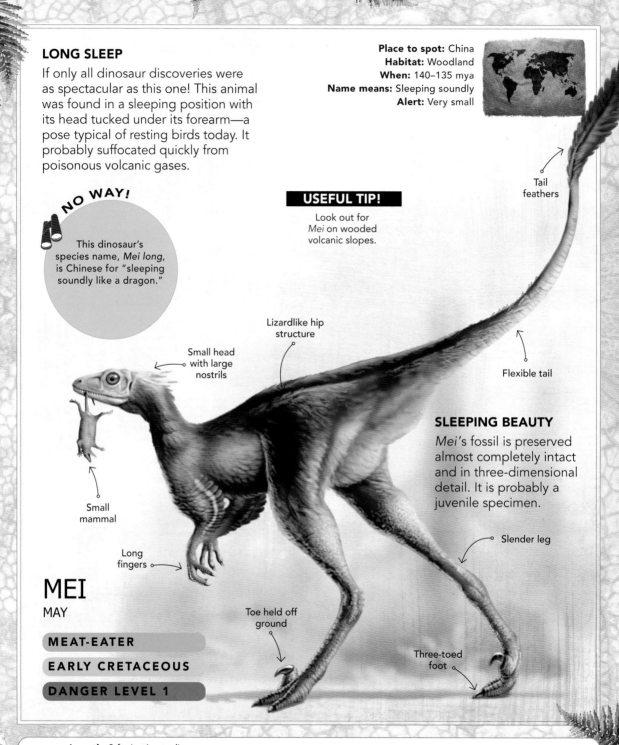

Tail feathers

Lizardlike hip structure

Small head with large nostrils

Flexible tail

SLEEPING BEAUTY

Mei's fossil is preserved almost completely intact and in three-dimensional detail. It is probably a juvenile specimen.

Small mammal

Slender leg

Long fingers

MEI
MAY

Toe held off ground

Three-toed foot

MEAT-EATER

EARLY CRETACEOUS

DANGER LEVEL 1

Length: 3 ft. (estimated)
Diet: Meat
Group: Theropoda
Family: Troodontidae

• The discoveries of *Mei* in a sleeping position and of the nesting oviraptosaur *Citipati* protecting a nest of eggs link theropod dinosaur behavior to living birds.

Place to spot: China
Habitat: Forest
When: 130–120 mya
Name means: Tiny thief
Alert: Swift glider

MICRORAPTOR
MY-kroh-RAP-tor

MEAT-EATER

EARLY CRETACEOUS

DANGER LEVEL 1

Fossil reveals trace of feather patterns

Shorter, downy feathers

Tail ends in diamond-shaped fan for stability

Long, iridescent feathers on hind leg

Three-toed feet

NO WAY!

In 2000, *Microraptor* was the first dinosaur to be discovered with feathers.

Three-fingered hand

TREE GLIDER

Microraptor probably glides from tree to tree like today's "flying" squirrels. Its legs may help to steer it through the air.

FEATHERED LEGS

The most unusual thing about this small dinosaur is its feathered hind limbs. The long and tapered feathers come from its thighbones and shinbones and make *Microraptor* look as if it has four wings. The "hind wings" may provide lifting power for true flight as well as gliding.

USEFUL TIP!

Look for *Microraptor* gliding between trees.

Length: 30 inches
Meat: Insects, lizards
Group: Theropoda
Family: Dromaeosauridae

• *Microraptor* is much more closely related to *Velociraptor* than to living birds, but its lifestyle suggests a form of movement that developed into the powered flight of birds.

MINMI
MIN-mee

PLANT-EATER

EARLY CRETACEOUS

DANGER LEVEL 2

Place to spot: Australia
Habitat: Open woodland
When: 119–113 mya
Name means: Lizard from Minmi Crossing
Alert: Sharp, thorny plates

SCUTES
The armor on its belly is made up of small, hexagonal, pebblelike bony plates called scutes.

USEFUL TIP!

This thorny customer browses in woodland.

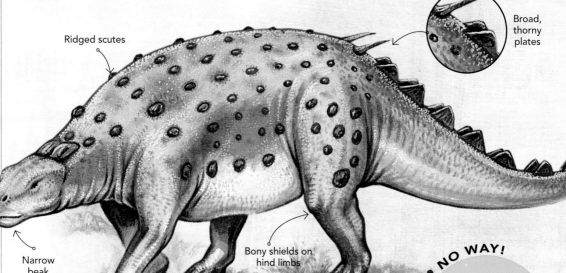

Ridged scutes

Broad, thorny plates

Narrow beak

Bony shields on hind limbs

Broad, sturdy foot

ARMORED STRIPS
This ankylosaur from Queensland, Australia, has a relatively light armor of boney scutes of various sizes and shapes, underlain by unique backbones. Unlike most other ankylosaurs, the scutes lie in rows from back to front.

NO WAY!

The fossilized content of *Minmi*'s gut has been found. It includes fruit and undigested seeds.

Length: 6–10 ft.
Diet: Low-growing plants
Group: Ankylosauria
Family: Ankylosauridae

• *Minmi* is smaller than other ankylosaurs and has such unusual armor that some scientists think that it may belong to a separate group of armored dinosaurs.

Place to spot: Mongolia
Habitat: Desert plains
When: 81–68 mya
Name means: Single (one) claw
Alert: Fast runner

MONONYKUS
mon-o-NY-kus

MEAT-EATER

LATE CRETACEOUS

DANGER LEVEL 1

Fused wrist bone

Claw

GRACEFUL RUNNER

Mononykus has graceful hind limbs for fast running, but its arms are extremely short and its hands consist of just a single digit—a clawed thumb.

Small head

Body covered in feathery down

Flexible vertebrae

Long tail

Single claw

SINGLE CLAWS

The unique feature of this bird-size theropod is the single claw on the end of each arm. Its arms are so short that the claws do not reach its mouth. These small arms may be used to dig into termite mounds. Its small teeth, which have no cutting edges, support this idea.

Long, skinny legs

Nimble feet for running

NO WAY!

Mononykus has large eyes. This may mean that it hunts insects at night, when it is cooler and there are fewer predators.

USEFUL TIP!

Spot this dinosaur darting across dry desert plains.

Three-toed foot

Length: 3 ft.
Diet: Insects, small animals
Group: Theropoda
Family: Alvarezsauridae

• *Mononykus* is a close relative of *Shuvuuia*, an alvarezsaurid that is covered in feathers. It is highly likely that *Mononykus* is also feathered.

STRANGE MIX

This large and unusual ornithopod from Australia has an expanded nose area, similar to a hadrosaur's, and probably has a thumb claw that is like an iguanodont's. However, it also has shearing teeth, unlike any other ornithopod.

Place to spot: Australia
Habitat: Woodland
When: 112–98 mya
Name means: Lizard from Muttaburra
Alert: Sharp beak

ALL FOURS

Muttaburrasaurus spends most of its time on all fours, but can flee predators by running on two legs.

Possible spikes on back

Bony lump on snout

Serrated beak

Strong legs

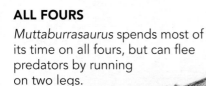

USEFUL TIP!

Its strong skull suggests that it prefers to eat tough plants.

MUTTABURRASAURUS

MUTT-uh-BUH-ruh-SAW-rus

PLANT-EATER

EARLY CRETACEOUS

DANGER LEVEL 3

Possible thumb spur

NO WAY!

Muttaburrasaurus can probably make loud calls using its hollow nose chamber.

Length: Up to 26 ft.
Diet: Tough plants
Group: Ornithopoda
Family: Rhabdodontidae

• The size and shape of *Muttaburrasaurus'* nose lump varies between individuals. Males and females probably have differently shaped lumps.

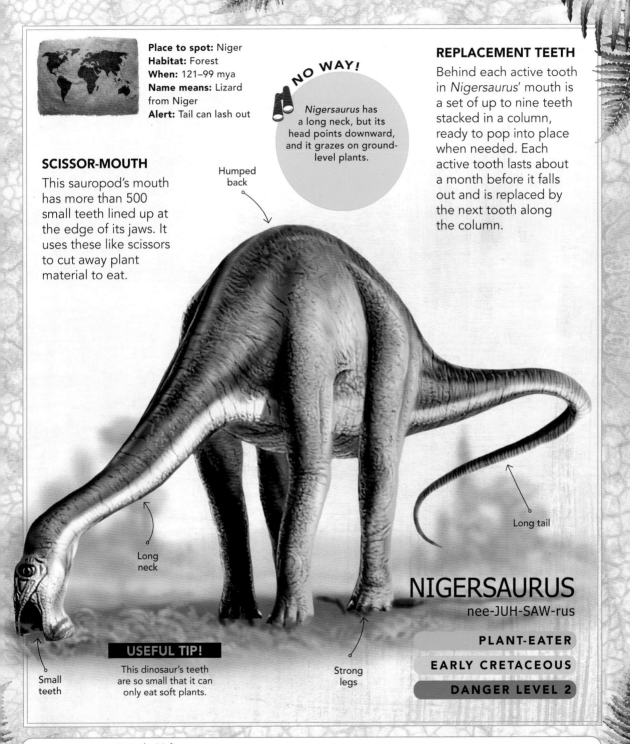

Place to spot: Niger
Habitat: Forest
When: 121–99 mya
Name means: Lizard from Niger
Alert: Tail can lash out

NO WAY!

Nigersaurus has a long neck, but its head points downward, and it grazes on ground-level plants.

REPLACEMENT TEETH

Behind each active tooth in *Nigersaurus'* mouth is a set of up to nine teeth stacked in a column, ready to pop into place when needed. Each active tooth lasts about a month before it falls out and is replaced by the next tooth along the column.

SCISSOR-MOUTH

This sauropod's mouth has more than 500 small teeth lined up at the edge of its jaws. It uses these like scissors to cut away plant material to eat.

Humped back

Long neck

Long tail

NIGERSAURUS
nee-JUH-SAW-rus

PLANT-EATER

EARLY CRETACEOUS

DANGER LEVEL 2

Small teeth

USEFUL TIP!

This dinosaur's teeth are so small that it can only eat soft plants.

Strong legs

Length: 50 ft.
Diet: Soft plants
Group: Sauropodomorpha
Family: Rebbachisauridae

• A full reconstruction of *Nigersaurus* has been made possible using the bones found in four separate, partially preserved fossils.

NOMINGIA
no-MING-ee-uh

MEAT-EATER

LATE CRETACEOUS

DANGER LEVEL 3

Place to spot: Mongolia
Habitat: Woodlands
When: 72–68 mya
Name means: From Nomingiin (in the Gobi Desert)
Alert: Large wing claws

NO WAY!

Some scientists believe *Nomingia* is a "missing link"—a dinosaur that was just about ready to fly like a bird.

USEFUL TIP!

The crest on its head is also used to attract mates.

Wing claws

End bones on tail are fused together

TAIL FEATHERS

Nomingia has a birdlike tail (pygostyle) of five fused vertebrae. The tail probably carries a fan of feathers used for display and to attract mates—much like a modern peacock's tail.

Strong legs

Beaked jaws

Soft feathers on body

RUNNING, NOT FLYING

Despite having feathers, wings, and a pygostyle, *Nomingia* is too heavy to fly. Instead, it runs after its prey, using its wings to help it to jump farther.

Long back claws

No feathers on foot

Length: 3–6 ft.
Diet: Meat
Group: Theropoda
Family: Oviraptoridae

• *Nomingia* was the first dinosaur to be discovered with a pygostyle, a feature common to all birds. However, *Nomingia* was a dinosaur, not a bird.

Place to spot: USA
Habitat: Forests
When: 156–145 mya
Name means: Bird robber
Alert: Quick runner

ORNITHOLESTES
ORN-ith-oh-LESS-tees

MEAT-EATER

LATE JURASSIC

DANGER LEVEL 2

NOSE CREST

The skull was once thought to have a bony crest, but this was probably caused by flattening during fossilization.

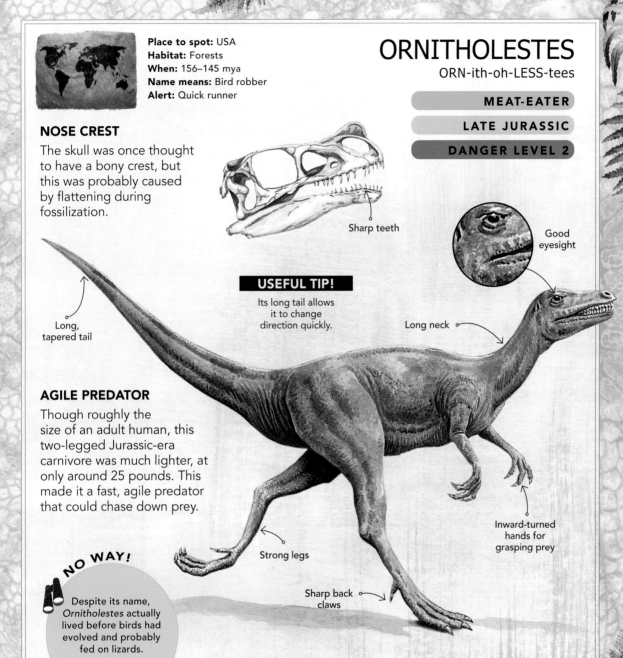

Sharp teeth

Good eyesight

USEFUL TIP!
Its long tail allows it to change direction quickly.

Long neck

Long, tapered tail

AGILE PREDATOR

Though roughly the size of an adult human, this two-legged Jurassic-era carnivore was much lighter, at only around 25 pounds. This made it a fast, agile predator that could chase down prey.

Inward-turned hands for grasping prey

Strong legs

NO WAY!
Despite its name, *Ornitholestes* actually lived before birds had evolved and probably fed on lizards.

Sharp back claws

Length: 6 feet
Diet: Meat
Group: Theropoda
Family: Undecided

• Most of what we know about *Ornitholestes* is based on just one skull and skeleton found more than 100 years ago. No more complete fossils have been found.

ORYCTODROMEUS
oh-RIK-to-DROM-ee-us

PLANT-EATER

LATE CRETACEOUS

DANGER LEVEL 1

Place to spot: USA
Habitat: Forests and plains
When: 99–94 mya
Name means: Digging runner
Alert: Digs burrows

BURROW DWELLER

This small dinosaur weighs only about 65 pounds. It was the first known dinosaur fossil to be found inside its burrow. Two juveniles were discovered with an adult, still inside the burrow, indicating that this family died together. It also confirms that adult *Oryctodromeus* care for their young.

USEFUL TIP!

Look for this creature in soft-earth banks.

Short head

Possible osteoderms

Long, stiff tail

Broad snout

NO WAY!

As a small herbivore, *Oryctodromeus* needs its burrow to hide from large theropod predators.

Curved hands for digging

Fourth toe

DIGGER

Oryctodromeus' arms and snout seem to be adapted for digging, but they are not as well adapted as those of burrowing animals today.

Length: 6 ft.
Diet: Leaves, twigs
Group: Ornithischia
Family: Ornithopoda

• *Oryctodromeus* probably shares its burrows with a range of other burrowers of the Late Cretaceous, including the shrewlike early mammals.

Place to spot: Niger
Habitat: River deltas
When: 112–110 mya
Name means: Brave lizard
Alert: Prominent sail

OURANOSAURUS
OO-RAN-oh-SAW-rus

PLANT-EATER

EARLY CRETACEOUS

DANGER LEVEL 2

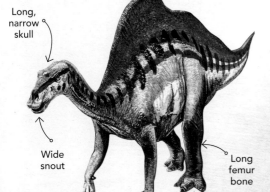

Long, narrow skull

Wide snout

Long femur bone

TALL SAIL

This ornithopod has a large "sail" on its back, made up of spines extending upward from the backbone. This sail is too fragile to protect the dinosaur, so it is probably used for display and temperature control.

SKULL

Ouranosaurus' long skull holds great dental weapons of 88 chewing teeth.

Tallest spines reach 2 feet high

Long neck

Thumb spike

Stiff tail

Strong legs support weight

NO WAY!

One theory argues that *Ouranosaurus'* spines hold a fatty lump of stored energy, similar to a bison's hump.

USEFUL TIP!

Look out for this animal near riverbanks.

Length: Up to 26 ft.
Diet: Leaves, fruit, seeds
Group: Ornithischia
Family: Iguanodontia

• If *Ouranosaurus* stands in the shade and its sail is wet, it will quickly radiate heat from the animal's enormous body.

OVIRAPTOR

oh-vee-RAP-tor

OMNIVORE

LATE CRETACEOUS

DANGER LEVEL 2

Places to spot: China, Mongolia
Habitat: Semi-desert
When: 85–75 mya
Name means: Egg thief
Alert: Fast runner

CREST

Dinosaur crests are varied and change constantly during the animal's lifetime.

WHOSE EGGS?

Oviraptor was named "egg thief" because the first one found seemed to be stealing a *Protoceratops* egg. In fact, *Oviraptor* was protecting its own eggs.

Beak and toothlike projections

Flexible neck

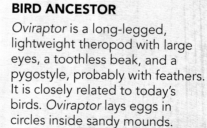

Bony crest

Sharply curved claws

Eggs arranged in a circle

NO WAY!

If a predator tries to steal an *Oviraptor* mother's eggs, she can scratch with her sharp claws or kick.

BIRD ANCESTOR

Oviraptor is a long-legged, lightweight theropod with large eyes, a toothless beak, and a pygostyle, probably with feathers. It is closely related to today's birds. *Oviraptor* lays eggs in circles inside sandy mounds.

USEFUL TIP!

Look for *Oviraptor* nests in sandy banks.

Length: Up to 6 ft.
Diet: Meat, fruit
Group: Theropoda
Family: Oviraptoridae

• Despite its birdlike appearance, certain signs—such as forward-pointing hip bones and a backward-pointing first toe—show that *Oviraptor* is not actually a bird.

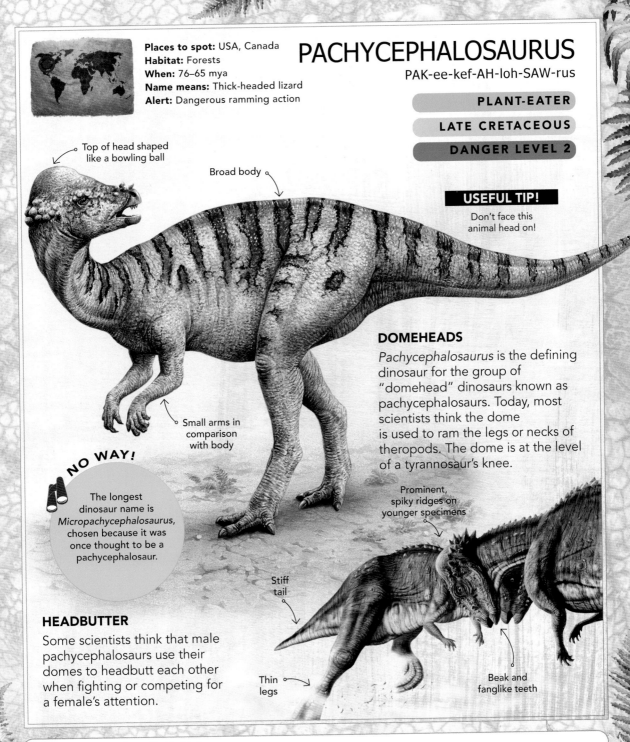

Places to spot: USA, Canada
Habitat: Forests
When: 76–65 mya
Name means: Thick-headed lizard
Alert: Dangerous ramming action

PACHYCEPHALOSAURUS

PAK-ee-kef-AH-loh-SAW-rus

PLANT-EATER

LATE CRETACEOUS

DANGER LEVEL 2

Top of head shaped like a bowling ball

Broad body

USEFUL TIP!

Don't face this animal head on!

Small arms in comparison with body

DOMEHEADS

Pachycephalosaurus is the defining dinosaur for the group of "domehead" dinosaurs known as pachycephalosaurs. Today, most scientists think the dome is used to ram the legs or necks of theropods. The dome is at the level of a tyrannosaur's knee.

NO WAY!

The longest dinosaur name is *Micropachycephalosaurus*, chosen because it was once thought to be a pachycephalosaur.

Prominent, spiky ridges on younger specimens

Stiff tail

HEADBUTTER

Some scientists think that male pachycephalosaurs use their domes to headbutt each other when fighting or competing for a female's attention.

Thin legs

Beak and fanglike teeth

Length: 10–16 ft.
Weight: Leaves, fruit
Group: Pachycephalosauria
Family: Pachycephalosauridae

• *Pachycephalosaurus'* neck vertebrae suggest that the animal's back has the ability to absorb shocks from the animal's ramming action.

TALKING TOGETHER

This hadrosaur uses the long, hollow crest on its head to make low-frequency sounds that can carry for many miles. It uses these calls to attract mates, to identify itself, and to convey information between herd members, such as "I found water" or "I just saw a tyrannosaur."

Places to spot: Canada, USA
Habitat: Woodlands
When: 76–74 mya
Name means: Near (like a) crested lizard
Alert: Lives in large herds

NO WAY!

It used to be thought that this dinosaur's crest was like a snorkel, letting it swim underwater. But there are no holes for it to breathe through!

Bony crest up to 6 feet long

Pebbly, textured skin

Tough, narrow beak

Strong throat for bellowing

THE CALL

When it calls, air enters the nose, travels around the hollow tube, and is then passed into the throat.

Pointy tail

PARASAUROLOPHUS
PAR-uh-SAW-roh-LOH-fus

PLANT-EATER

LATE CRETACEOUS

DANGER LEVEL 2

Walks on both hind feet and all fours

Webbed fingers

USEFUL TIP!

It's almost identical to the *Charonosaurus* from Asia.

Length: Up to 36 ft.
Diet: Pine needles, leaves
Group: Ornithischia
Family: Hadrosauridae

• *Parasaurolophus* was first discovered in Alberta, Canada, in 1920, and three species have since been identified.

Place to spot: Spain
Habitat: Plains and lakes
When: 133–130 mya
Name means: Pelican mimic
Alert: Lots of teeth

PELECANIMIMUS
pel-ee-KAN-i-MY-mus

MEAT-EATER

EARLY CRETACEOUS

DANGER LEVEL 2

NO WAY!

Pelecanimimus has more teeth than any other theropod yet discovered—even more than *Tyrannosaurus rex*.

Distinctive short crest

Narrow, lightweight body

Thin tail

Neck pouch for storing food

BIG SMILE

This unusual ornithomimosaur —one of a group of fast ostrichlike dinosaurs—has more than 220 small teeth. Most dinosaurs in this group have no teeth at all. *Pelecanimimus* teeth act like a fine cutting tool and filter food from the water. This dinosaur also has a strong tongue.

PELICAN POUCH

One of the most prominent features of *Pelecanimimus* is the unusual skin folds underneath its throat. These form a pouch, similar to that of a pelican, where it stores food.

Three long fingers used together as a claw

Birdlike feet

USEFUL TIP!

It eats a mixed diet of fish, small animals, and insects.

Length: Up to 8 ft.
Diet: Meat, fish
Group: Theropoda
Family: Ornithomimosauria

• Discovered in Spain in 1993, the fossil of *Pelecanimimus* includes the skull, much of the skeleton, and some skin impressions.

USEFUL TIP!

This dinosaur is not as slow as it looks!

Thick, long neck

Places to spot: Germany, Greenland, Norway
Habitat: Floodplains
When: 214–204 mya
Name means: Broad lizard
Alert: Very big

NO WAY!

This sauropod's thumb spike is large enough to stab attacking theropods. It is probably held off the ground.

Long skull with short teeth

Five-fingered hands with claws and thumb spike

PLATEOSAURUS
PLAY-tee-oh-SAW-rus

OMNIVORE

LATE TRIASSIC

DANGER LEVEL 2

EARLY SAUROPOD

Plateosaurus is a prosauropod—one of the first giant sauropods. Its teeth are designed for eating plants, but they are thick enough for the occasional meal of small animals. Its eyes are directed to the sides, rather than to the front, providing all-round vision for spotting any predators.

Length: 16–33 ft.
Diet: Leaves, small animals
Group: Prosauropoda
Family: Plateosauridae

• *Plateosaurus'* hands, with their five clawed fingers, could not be turned palm down for walking, so the animal must have moved around on its hind legs.

Places to spot: Canada, USA
Habitat: Swamps and floodplains
When: 77–75 mya
Name means: Before saurolophus
(Lizard crest)
Alert: Large herd animal

NO WAY!

As with *Saurolophus*, *Prosaurolophus* may have inflatable, soft-tissue sacs near its nostrils for making a sound display.

SOCIAL BEHAVIOUR

Bone-bed remains suggest that these dinosaurs gather around water holes during the dry season and may die together during severe droughts.

Tendons in back support heavy tail

Deep, "V"-shaped curve in spine

USEFUL TIP!

Look for these animals in or near forests, roaming in herds.

Jaw contains hundreds of teeth

Stiff, narrow tail

Stout, powerful hindlimbs

Slim forelimbs

PROSAUROLOPHUS
PRO-saw-ROL-oh-fus

DUCK BILL

This duck-billed dinosaur is known from several complete skulls and skeletons. It has a solid crest and is closely related to *Saurolophus*.

PLANT-EATER

LATE CRETACEOUS

DANGER LEVEL 2

Length: Up to 30 ft.
Diet: Leaves, twigs
Group: Ornithopoda
Family: Hadrosauridae

• *Prosaurolphus* crops plants with its beak and chews them in dental batteries containing hundreds of teeth that are continually replaced.

PROTOCERATOPS
PRO-toe-SER-a-tops

PLANT-EATER

LATE CRETACEOUS

DANGER LEVEL 2

Places to spot: China, Mongolia
Habitat: Open woodland
When: 86–71 mya
Name means: First horned face
Alert: Sharp beak

Frill

HORNLESS FRILL
The dinosaur has a well-developed frill that extends back from its face and over its neck. It does not have large horns.

Narrow beak

SHARP BEAK
Protoceratops has a parrotlike beak that shears off plants, and scissorlike teeth that slice up its food.

Broad feet

Spadelike claws for digging

FIGHT TO THE END
Here, *Velociraptor* battles with *Protoceratops*, squashing some dinosaur eggs in the process. *Protoceratops* is biting its opponent's arm.

Velociraptor

NO WAY!
Fossils of a *Velociraptor* and a *Protoceratops* have been found locked together in a deadly fight.

USEFUL TIP!
Males have larger frills than females.

Protoceratops

Length: Up to 6 ft.
Diet: Plants
Group: Ceratopsia
Family: Protoceratopsidae

• This ceratopsian is known from hundreds of complete skulls and many skeletons. So many skulls have been found in the Gobi Desert that an entire series of specimens, from egg to adult, has been studied.

Places to spot: China, Mongolia, Thailand, Russia
Habitat: Woodland
When: 120 mya
Name means: Parrot lizard
Alert: Sharp claws

MANY SPECIES

This small ceratopsian walks on both two and four legs. It has a parrotlike beak, and its teeth can chop plants but not chew them. Many fossils of *Psittacosaurus* have been found, and scientists have identified 14 different species by comparing the shape of the skulls.

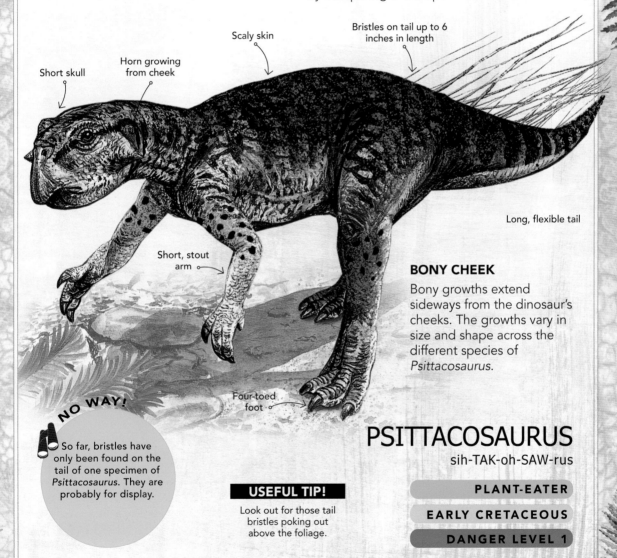

Scaly skin

Bristles on tail up to 6 inches in length

Short skull

Horn growing from cheek

Long, flexible tail

Short, stout arm

BONY CHEEK

Bony growths extend sideways from the dinosaur's cheeks. The growths vary in size and shape across the different species of *Psittacosaurus*.

Four-toed foot

NO WAY!

So far, bristles have only been found on the tail of one specimen of *Psittacosaurus*. They are probably for display.

USEFUL TIP!

Look out for those tail bristles poking out above the foliage.

PSITTACOSAURUS
sih-TAK-oh-SAW-rus

PLANT-EATER

EARLY CRETACEOUS

DANGER LEVEL 1

Length: 6 ft.
Diet: Tough plants
Group: Ceratopsia
Family: Psittacosauridae

• More than 400 fossils of *Psittacosaurus* have been dug up. One adult fossil has been found with 30 babies in tow.

OUT IN THE COLD

This little plant-eater lives at the southern end of the supercontinent of Gondwana (in what is now Australia) in the Antarctic Circle. It spends a few months each year in "polar night," when it stays dark for 24 hours.

Place to spot: Australia
Habitat: Woodlands
When: 115 mya
Name means: Qantas (Australian airline) lizard
Alert: Excellent eyesight

NO WAY!

It feeds on ferns, which it reduces to pulp using its muscular cheeks and ridged teeth.

Long, high tail

Large eyes adapted for low light

Squat, powerful thighs

Beak-like mouth

FINDING ITS WAY

Qantassaurus has large eyes to help it see in the dark. It's warm blooded, staying active all year round rather than hibernating.

Short, stubby fingers

Long shins for fast running

USEFUL TIP!

Beware—this dinosaur may spot you first!

Claws for gripping ground

QANTASSAURUS
KWON-tuh-SAW-rus

PLANT-EATER

EARLY CRETACEOUS

DANGER LEVEL 2

Length: Up to 6 ft.
Diet: Plants
Group: Ornithischia
Family: Ornithopoda

• *Qantassaurus* was named after an Australian airline that has provided financial support for dinosaur research.

Place to spot: Niger
Habitat: Woodlands
When: 95 mya
Name means: Wrinkle face
Alert: Scavenges on dead creatures

RUGOPS
ROO-gops

MEAT-EATER

MID-CRETACEOUS

DANGER LEVEL 3

Bones on top of head

Long tail

Short arms

Large, powerful feet

OUT ON DISPLAY

This dinosaur has many pointy bones on top of its nose and between its eyes. These are used for display against rivals rather than for fighting.

USEFUL TIP!

Stay away when it's feeding—it might attack you.

SCAVENGER

Rugops has a short, wide skull with jaws that are too weak for active hunting. Instead, it scavenges, eating the remains of dead dinosaurs and other creatures.

NO WAY!

Rugops may look fierce and threatening, but it has small teeth and short arms.

Length: Up to 15 ft.
Diet: Meat
Group: Theropoda
Family: Abelisauridae

• So far, only a single skull of *Rugops* has been discovered. Scientists estimate that the dinosaur would have weighed 1,000 pounds.

SALTASAURUS
SALT-ah-SAW-rus

PLANT-EATER

LATE CRETACEOUS

DANGER LEVEL 2

Places to spot: Argentina, Uruguay
Habitat: Lowlands
When: 70–65 mya
Name means: Lizard from Salta
Alert: Lightly armored back

PROTECTIVE SCUTES
The bony scutes on *Saltasaurus'* back are small, but just big enough to break an attacking theropod's teeth.

Small brain

Bony scutes form a tough armor

Neck tendons mean that the head is kept fairly low

Muscular tail helps dinosaur to rear up on its hind legs

SHORT SAUROPOD
This short, stocky sauropod lives in South America in Late Cretaceous times. It is one of the earliest sauropods known to have bony lumps in its skin along both sides of its backbone.

USEFUL TIP!

Look for *Saltasaurus* browsing tree leaves.

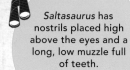

NO WAY!

Saltasaurus has nostrils placed high above the eyes and a long, low muzzle full of teeth.

Length: 40 ft.
Diet: Ferns, leaves
Group: Sauropodomorpha
Family: Saltasauridae

• Bony neck tendons mean that *Saltasaurus* cannot raise its head above shoulder height, so it browses on ferns and low-hanging branches.

Places to spot: Canada, Mongolia
Habitat: Forests
When: 69 mya
Name means: Lizard crest, or ridged lizard
Alert: Very big

SAUROLOPHUS
SAW-roh-LOW-fus

PLANT-EATER

LATE CRETACEOUS

DANGER LEVEL 2

DINO CALL

This duck-billed dinosaur can walk on two or four legs. It has a solid bony spike projecting from the back of the skull, which may support a crest of skin along the neck, and an inflatable sac of skin on the nose for call sounds.

Backbone curves down sharply at shoulders

Stiff, narrow tail

Nostril openings

USEFUL TIP!

Can be heard calling near swamps and rivers.

Bony beak

NO WAY!

Until a fossilized skin sac is discovered, scientists will not know for sure what sort of sound *Saurolophus* made.

PLANT-MUNCHER

Behind its bony beak, *Saurolophus* has tightly packed teeth for grinding up tough plants.

Shortened forelimbs

Length: 30–40 ft.
Diet: Ferns, pine needles
Group: Ornithopoda
Family: Hadrosauridae

• Hadrosaurs such as *Saurolophus* are among the largest dinosaurs of the Cretaceous and are preyed upon by tyrannosaurs and other theropods.

SCELIDOSAURUS
SKEL-ee-do-SAW-rus

PLANT-EATER

EARLY JURASSIC

DANGER LEVEL 2

Place to spot: England
Habitat: Woodland
When: 206–191 mya
Name means: Rib lizard
Alert: Short, stocky and strong

Bony plates embedded in the dinosaur's skin

NO WAY!
It was named by Richard Owen, who also came up with the word "dinosaur," in 1842.

FIRST ARMOR

Scelidosaurus was one of the earliest armored dinosaurs to appear on Earth.

Short neck for an armored dinosaur

Parallel rows of plates

Mouth filled with leaf-shaped teeth

BUMPY BODY

Scelidosaurus has parallel rows of small, bony bumps in its skin all the way down its body and tail. A four–legged herbivore, its back legs are longer than it front legs.

Shorter front legs than back

USEFUL TIP!
It can rear up on its back legs to eat high vegetation.

Length: Up to 13 ft.
Diet: Plants
Group: Ornithischia
Family: Scelidosauridae

• Found in the crumbling Jurassic–period cliffs of Dorset, England, *Scelidosaurus* was until recently the most complete dinosaur fossil ever found in the UK.

Place to spot: Italy
Habitat: Lagoons
When: 120–110 mya
Name means: Scipio claw
Alert: Quick and agile

SCIPIONYX
SHIH-pee-OH-niks

MEAT-EATER

EARLY CRETACEOUS

DANGER LEVEL 2

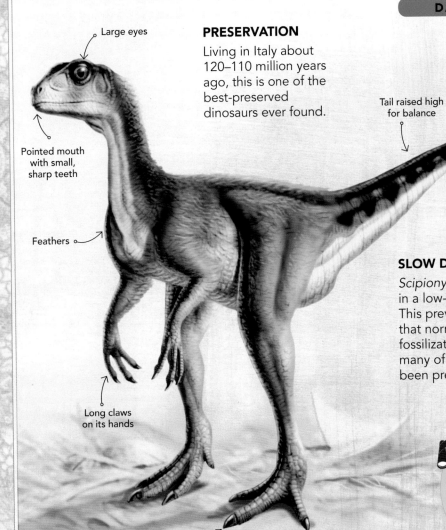

Large eyes

PRESERVATION

Living in Italy about 120–110 million years ago, this is one of the best-preserved dinosaurs ever found.

Pointed mouth with small, sharp teeth

Feathers

Long claws on its hands

Three-toed back foot

Tail raised high for balance

USEFUL TIP!

It feeds on insects, small birds, and fish.

SLOW DECAY

Scipionyx was buried in mud in a low-oxygen environment. This prevented the decay that normally occurs during fossilization. As a result, many of its soft tissues have been preserved.

NO WAY!

This is the only dinosaur ever discovered with fossilized traces of its intestines, liver, windpipe, and some of its muscles still preserved.

Length: 6 ft.
Diet: Meat, fish
Group: Theropoda
Family: Compsognathidae

• The only known fossil of *Scipionyx* is believed to be a baby. It's one of only a few dinosaurs ever to be found in Italy.

SCUTELLOSAURUS

skoo-TELL-oh-SAW-rus

PLANT-EATER

EARLY JURASSIC

DANGER LEVEL 1

Place to spot: USA
Habitat: Woodlands
When: 205–202 mya
Name means: Little shield lizard
Alert: Well protected

EARLY WALKER

This dinosaur is an early, and rather unusual, ornithischian. Later dinosaurs of this type are large and walk on four legs, but *Scutellosaurus* is small—about the size of a dog—and walks on two legs.

Triangular back plates

Bony plates

Side-facing eyes for spotting predators

BONY PLATES

Scutellosaurus is covered in hundreds of flat, bony plates for protection. It also has tall, triangular plates running down its spine and tail.

Strong front limbs for tearing vegetation

Sharp back claws

NO WAY!

Its hard plates can break attackers' teeth, while its long tail can be used as a whip.

USEFUL TIP!

Its neck, back, ribs, and tail are covered in bony plates.

Length: 4 ft.
Diet: Plants
Group: Ornithischia
Family: Thyreophora

• *Scutellosaurus* is one of the earliest armored dinosaurs and an ancestor of the much larger armored dinosaurs, such as *Stegosaurus* and *Ankylosaurus*.

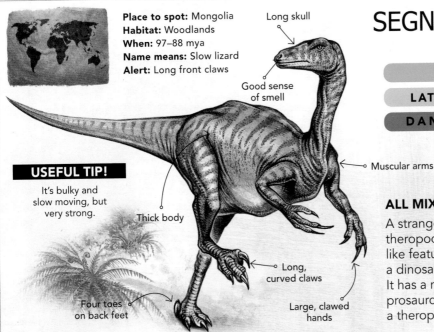

Place to spot: Mongolia
Habitat: Woodlands
When: 97–88 mya
Name means: Slow lizard
Alert: Long front claws

Long skull

Good sense of smell

SEGNOSAURUS
SEG-noh-SAW-rus

MEAT-EATER

LATE CRETACEOUS

DANGER LEVEL 3

Muscular arms

USEFUL TIP!

It's bulky and slow moving, but very strong.

Thick body

ALL MIXED UP

A strange mixture of theropod's and prosauropod-like features, *Segnosaurus* is a dinosaur unlike any other. It has a narrow beak, like a prosauropod's, but teeth like a theropod's.

Long, curved claws

Large, clawed hands

Four toes on back feet

Place to spot: USA
Habitat: Desert plains
When: 201–196 mya
Name means: A mythical sand monster
Alert: Large thumb claw

STRONG LEGS

Unlike its sauropod descendants, this dinosaur can walk on two legs. *Seitaad* uses them to wander the white sand dunes of its desert habitat searching for plants it can eat.

USEFUL TIP!

Watch out for the large, twisted thumb spike it uses for feeding and perhaps defense.

Thick arms

SEITAAD
SAY-ee-TAH-ad

PLANT-EATER

EARLY JURASSIC

DANGER LEVEL 3

Large thumb claw for feeding

Strong legs for walking

Length: 13–20 ft. (estimated)
Diet: Meat
Group: Theropoda
Family: Therizinosauridae

Length: 15 ft.
Diet: Plants
Group: Sauropodomorpha
Family: Massospondylidae

SHUNOSAURUS
SHOO-no-SAW-rus

PLANT-EATER

MID-JURASSIC

DANGER LEVEL 3

Place to spot: China
Habitat: Plains
When: 170–160 mya
Name means: Lizard from Shu
Alert: Dangerous tail

SAUROPOD ANCESTOR
An early, primitive form of sauropod, *Shunosaurus* roams the Chinese plains in large herds. It has a very short neck compared to later sauropods.

Tail much longer than neck

Flexible tail

Mouth contains both round and spoonlike teeth

Club at end of tail

Front legs shorter than back legs

NO WAY!
Shunosaurus has more teeth than any other known sauropod.

USEFUL TIP!
Steer clear – adults can weigh up to 3 tons.

CLUBBED AWAY
Shunosaurus' tail ends in a large, bony club, which it uses to defend itself against predators.

Length: Up to 33 ft.
Diet: Plants
Group: Saurischia
Family: Cetiosauridae

• More than 20 nearly complete *Shunosaurus* skeletons have been excavated in China, making it one of the best-understood sauropods.

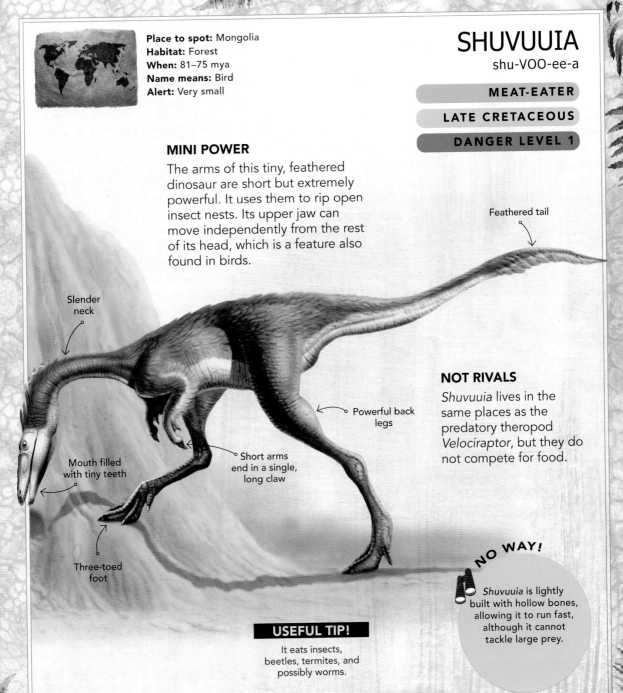

Place to spot: Mongolia
Habitat: Forest
When: 81–75 mya
Name means: Bird
Alert: Very small

SHUVUUIA
shu-VOO-ee-a

MEAT-EATER
LATE CRETACEOUS
DANGER LEVEL 1

MINI POWER

The arms of this tiny, feathered dinosaur are short but extremely powerful. It uses them to rip open insect nests. Its upper jaw can move independently from the rest of its head, which is a feature also found in birds.

Feathered tail

Slender neck

Powerful back legs

NOT RIVALS

Shuvuuia lives in the same places as the predatory theropod *Velociraptor*, but they do not compete for food.

Mouth filled with tiny teeth

Short arms end in a single, long claw

Three-toed foot

NO WAY!

Shuvuuia is lightly built with hollow bones, allowing it to run fast, although it cannot tackle large prey.

USEFUL TIP!

It eats insects, beetles, termites, and possibly worms.

Length: 2 ft.
Diet: Meat
Group: Theropoda
Family: Alvarezsauridae

• Two skulls and some skeleton bones of *Shuvuuia* have been discovered so far in the Gobi Desert, Mongolia.

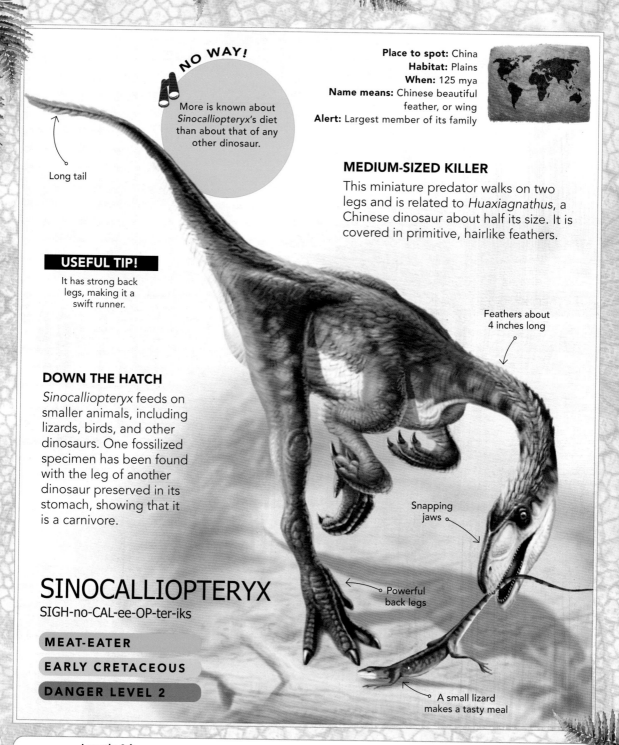

NO WAY!

More is known about *Sinocalliopteryx*'s diet than about that of any other dinosaur.

Long tail

Place to spot: China
Habitat: Plains
When: 125 mya
Name means: Chinese beautiful feather, or wing
Alert: Largest member of its family

MEDIUM-SIZED KILLER

This miniature predator walks on two legs and is related to *Huaxiagnathus*, a Chinese dinosaur about half its size. It is covered in primitive, hairlike feathers.

USEFUL TIP!

It has strong back legs, making it a swift runner.

Feathers about 4 inches long

DOWN THE HATCH

Sinocalliopteryx feeds on smaller animals, including lizards, birds, and other dinosaurs. One fossilized specimen has been found with the leg of another dinosaur preserved in its stomach, showing that it is a carnivore.

Snapping jaws

SINOCALLIOPTERYX
SIGH-no-CAL-ee-OP-ter-iks

Powerful back legs

MEAT-EATER

EARLY CRETACEOUS

DANGER LEVEL 2

A small lizard makes a tasty meal

Length: 8 ft.
Diet: Meat
Group: Theropoda
Family: Compsognathidae

• Scientists believe *Sinocalliopteryx* stalks and ambushes its prey, much like a modern cat does. One specimen has the remains of two birds in its stomach.

Place to spot: China
Habitat: Forests
When: 124–120 mya
Name means: Chinese bird lizard
Alert: Large, sharp claws

SINORNITHOSAURUS
SIGH-nor-nith-oh-SAW-rus

MEAT-EATER

EARLY CRETACEOUS

DANGER LEVEL 3

USEFUL TIP!

Resembles the earlier dinosaur *Archaeopteryx*.

Grooved teeth

Long wing feathers

Sharp, curved claws

FEATHER TYPES

This small predator has many different types of feathers, including downlike tufts, body feathers, and primitive flight feathers on its arms.

Raised claw on back foot

Downlike feathers on legs

NO WAY!

Some scientists used to believe *Sinornithosaurus* has a venomous bite that it uses to paralyze its prey.

CAMOUFLAGE

According to fossilized pigments, *Sinornithosaurus'* feathers are colored reddish-brown, yellow, and black. These colors help to camouflage the dinosaur, allowing it to blend in with the Cretaceous forests where it hunts its prey.

Length: 3–6 ft.
Diet: Meat
Group: Theropoda
Family: Dromaeosauridae

• An almost complete fossil skeleton of *Sinornithosaurus* was found in 1999 by Xu Xing, one of the most famous Chinese paleontologists.

SINOSAUROPTERYX

SIGH-no-saw-ROP-ter-iks

MEAT-EATER

EARLY CRETACEOUS

DANGER LEVEL 1

Place to spot: China
Habitat: Woodlands
When: 122–120 mya
Name means: Chinese lizard wing
Alert: Jaws can deliver a painful nip

FEATHERED FIEND

Sinosauropteryx is a small theropod from the Cretaceous period. Its body is covered in thin, hollow, featherlike filaments that keep it warm, although it cannot fly.

NO WAY!

Sinosauropteryx has the longest tail, relative to its size, of any theropod.

Extremely
long tail

Mouth filled
with small,
sharp teeth

Long first finger

Strong rear feet
for quick running

USEFUL TIP!

It preys on small lizards
and mammals.

SHORT ARMS

Sinosauropteryx has a long tail but very short arms—just a third the length of its legs.

Length: 3 ft.
Diet: Meat
Group: Theropoda
Family: Compsognathidae

• Some *Sinosauropteryx* fossils have been found with traces of color. As a result, we know the dinosaur has a stripy tail, dark top, and light underside.

Place to spot: China
Habitat: Forests and plains
When: 130–125 mya
Name means: Chinese hunter
Alert: Crafty and cunning

SINOVENATOR
SIGH-no-ven-NAY-tor

OMNIVORE

EARLY CRETACEOUS

DANGER LEVEL 1

EARLY BIRD

About the size of a chicken, this is one of the earliest birdlike dinosaurs, or troodonts. It has long legs and short arms and is covered in feathers. Like the *Sinosauropteryx*, it cannot fly.

Small head

Very long tail

Feeding on an egg

NO WAY!

As well as hunting small creatures, it probably also scavenges eggs and dead animals as part of its diet.

Nest raided for its eggs

Long, thin back legs

Raised claw on each back foot

SMALL PREY

Unlike its larger, more famous relative, *Troodon*, *Sinovenator* does not have sawlike bumps on its teeth for tearing the flesh of large animals. Instead, it feeds on smaller lizards and insects.

USEFUL TIP!

It is hunted by other, larger dinosaurs.

Length: Up to 3 ft.
Diet: Meat, plants
Group: Theropoda
Family: Troodontidae

• With some characteristics of troodons and some of raptors, *Sinovenator* shows a close relationship between these two groups.

SINRAPTOR

sin-RAP-tor

MEAT-EATER

LATE JURASSIC

DANGER LEVEL 5

Place to spot: China
Habitat: Woodlands
When: 169–142 mya
Name means: Chinese robber
Alert: Ferocious hunter

NO WAY!

The "Sin" part of its name means that it was found in China, not that it was evil.

Head about 3 feet long

BIG BOY

This big Jurassic meat-eater is one of the first fossils found that featured teeth marks from another predator, possibly even from another *Sinraptor*.

Spines along back

Powerful neck

Tail as long as its body

Three claws on its front legs

Large, tearing claws on back legs

USEFUL TIP!

It preys on young sauropods.

FIGHT!

Sinraptors fight each other using their long, sharp teeth. These fights are dramatic and bloody.

Length: 25 ft.
Diet: Meat
Group: Theropoda
Family: Metriacanthosauridae

• Sauropod bones have been discovered bearing the bite marks of hungry *Sinraptor*.

Place to spot: China
Habitat: Forests and plains
When: 89–65 mya
Name means: Lizard from Sonid
Alert: Covered in bony plates

SONIDOSAURUS
SON-id-oh-SAW-rus

PLANT-EATER

LATE CRETACEOUS

DANGER LEVEL 2

Long neck for reaching the tops of tall plants

BONY PLATES

This is an early type of titanosaur, a group of sauropods with bony plates on their skin.

USEFUL TIP!

It is one of the smaller sauropods.

Spines pointing up from backbone

Protective plates on back

ALL MIXED UP

Not a lot is known about this dinosaur. It appears to have a mixture of features from early and later titanosaurs. Like all sauropods, *Sonidosaurus* has a long neck and tail. But it also has a row of thick spines poking straight up from its backbone.

Thin tail

NO WAY!

Some palaeontologists believe *Sonidosaurus* evolved in Asia, away from the main group of titanosaurs.

Length: 30 ft.
Diet: Plants
Group: Sauropodomorpha
Family: Titanosauria

• *Sonidosaurus* is known from one partial skeleton made up of just a few back, hip, tail, and rib bones.

SPINOSAURUS

SPY-noh-SAW-rus

MEAT-EATER

LATE CRETACEOUS

DANGER LEVEL 5

Place to spot: Egypt
Habitat: Coastal areas
When: 112–97 mya
Name means: Spine lizard
Alert: Massive spiny "sail"

UNUSUAL THEROPOD

Spinosaurs are unusual theropods with crocodile-like skulls and "sails" on their backs. *Spinosaurus* has long hands with long, curved claws. It may use its claws to hunt fish.

USEFUL TIP!

Can be spotted eating along beaches.

Sail reaches more than 6 feet in height

Neck less strongly curved than other theropods'

Deep, narrow tail with powerful muscles at base

Hands with long claws

Three long, forward-facing toes

SAIL

Scientists believe this is a swimming dinosaur that uses its sail to steer as it swims toward prey. It uses its neck and tail to stun the prey before eating it.

NO WAY!

The best *Spinosaurus* skeleton was destroyed by a bombing raid on Germany in World War II.

Length: 49–52 ft.
Diet: Fish, meat
Group: Theropoda
Family: Spinosauridae

• At up to 52 feet in length and more than 7.7 tons in weight, *Spinosaurus* is massive—possibly the largest meat-eater that has ever walked on Earth.

Place to spot: USA
Habitat: Open woodland
When: 156–144 mya
Name means: Covered lizard
Alert: Swinging spiked tail

PLANT-CROPPER

Stegosaurus has a sharp beak that it uses to crop food like a pair of shears.

USEFUL TIP!

This dino may be slow, but beware its spikes!

17 large plates

Small head

Short forelegs allow for browsing among low plants

PLATES

Stegosaurus' plates are used for display and to keep it cool, as well as for defense.

HEAVY ARMOR

Stegosaurus is an armor-plated dinosaur that can defend itself against big predators. It has 17 tall plates and four tail spikes. It cannot run at all, which is why it relies on defense.

NO WAY!

Despite being 30 feet long and weighing about 4.9 tons, *Stegosaurus'* brain is only the size of a small orange.

STEGOSAURUS
STEG-oh-SAW-rus

PLANT-EATER

LATE JURASSIC

DANGER LEVEL 3

Length: 30 ft.
Diet: Ferns, shrubs
Group: Thyreophora
Family: Stegosauridae

• *Stegosaurus* is covered in armor. Even its throat is protected by more than 100 small bones embedded in the skin.

STRUTHIOMIMUS
STROOTH-ee-oh-MY-muss

OMNIVORE

LATE CRETACEOUS

DANGER LEVEL 2

Places to spot: Canada, USA
Habitat: Plains
When: 76–74 mya
Name means: Ostrich mimic
Alert: Only tackles small prey

NO WAY!

Scientists think that *Struthiomimus* may be able to run at speeds of up to 50 mph.

FAST RUNNER

Struthiomimus is an ostrichlike dinosaur. It has large eyes, thin arms, and long legs, which allow it to run very fast.

Tail for balance

Long neck

Toothless mouth

Thin arms

Powerful leg muscles for running quickly

Narrow feet

LITTLE FEEDER

Struthiomimus has weak jaws without any teeth and its hands are hooklike. Its arms cannot reach up or down, so it eats plant food at shoulder height, as well as possibly small animals.

USEFUL TIP!

It may hunt at night as well as during the day.

Length: Up to 14 ft.
Diet: Meat and plants
Group: Theropoda
Family: Ornithomimidae

• Many specimens of *Struthiomimus* have been discovered at the famous Dinosaur Provincial Park, a major hunting ground for fossils in Alberta, Canada.

Places to spot: Canada, USA
Habitat: Open woodland
When: 76–70 mya
Name means: Spiked lizard
Alert: Spiky frill

STYRACOSAURUS
sty-RACK-oh-SAW-rus

PLANT-EATER

LATE CRETACEOUS

DANGER LEVEL 2

Long horn for defense

Long frill spikes for defense and display

SPIKY DINO

Styracosaurus belongs to a group of ceratopsians known as centrosaurines. Their frills are decorated with spikes, knobs, and hooks. The nose horn tends to be larger.

Holes in frill bone reduce its weight

Curved, toothless beak

NO WAY!

Styracosaurus' nose horn is long enough to stab right through a theropod's leg.

DEFENSE

Styracosaurus' spiky frill protects its neck. Its huge, sharp nose horn can rip open a predator's belly.

USEFUL TIP!

Don't get in front of this animal. It may charge!

Length: 18 ft.
Diet: Ferns, cycads
Group: Ceratopsia
Family: Ceratopsidae

• The bulky body of *Styracosaurus* resembles that of the rhinoceros. It has powerful shoulders, and males may fight over females.

TALENKAUEN

TAH-len-KOW-en

PLANT-EATER

LATE CRETACEOUS

DANGER LEVEL 1

Place to spot: Argentina
Habitat: Forest
When: 70–65 mya
Name means: Small skull
Alert: Fast runner

USEFUL TIP!

Don't frighten this
dinosaur. It will run
away fast!

THIN ARMOR

This ornithopod lives at the end of
the Cretaceous, but looks more like
a Jurassic ornithopod. It has small,
overlapping, eight-inch-thick armored
plates across its ribs, which are too thin
to serve as a defense against predators.

Small skull

Long, slender
neck

Four-fingered
hands

Long tail for
balance

Long, slender
legs for
running

NO WAY!

Other ornithopods,
such as *Hypsilophodon*,
have egg-shaped plates
like those of *Talenkauen*.
Their true purpose
is unknown.

FAST RUNNER

Talenkauen has long legs and a light
build—its main defense is the speed
at which it can outrun predators.

Length: Up to 13 ft.
Diet: Ferns, shrubs
Group: Ornithopoda
Family: Iguanodontia

• *Talenkauen* was found in a rock formation with raptor and
tyrannosaurid remains nearby. These may be *Talenkauen*'s predators.

Places to spot: USA, Canada
Habitat: Subtropical swamps
When: 120–110 mya
Name means: Sinew lizard
Alert: Dangerous kick

TENONTOSAURUS
ten-ON-toh-SAW-rus

PLANT-EATER

EARLY CRETACEOUS

DANGER LEVEL 2

ALL FOURS

This animal walks on four legs, but rears up on its back legs when feeding or fighting.

Specialized tendons in hips help suspend long tail

Narrow, deep skull

Bony, beaklike mouth

NO WAY!

For protection, *Tenontosaurus'* young stay with their parents after hatching.

Four pointed feet have a dangerous kick

RAPTOR PREY

This ornithopod is most famous for being the prey of *Deinonychus*. Remains of *Tenontosaurus* have often been found with *Deinonychus* skeletons nearby. *Deinonychus* may attack young *Tenontosaurus* rather than the adults, and deadly fights may break out with the predators.

USEFUL TIP!

If you see this dino, beware! A pack of *Deinonychus* may be nearby.

Length: 21–26 ft.
Diet: Ferns, cycads
Group: Ornithopoda
Family: Iguanodontia

• *Tenontosaurus* browses on ground-level shrubs, but its hard beak means that it can crop even the toughest plants.

NO WAY!

Places to spot: Canada, USA
Habitat: Forest
When: 67–65 mya
Name means: Pierced lizard
Alert: Giant head and horns

Some scientists argue that *Torosaurus* and *Triceratops* are the same dinosaur, but at different stages of growth.

USEFUL TIP!

Can be spotted in large herds.

Elongated frill with large openings in the bone

Very long and sharp bony spikes

Short nose horn

Relatively long tail

Very sturdy legs

Beaked mouth contains shearing cheek teeth

TOROSAURUS
TOR-oh-SAW-rus

PLANT-EATER

LATE CRETACEOUS

DANGER LEVEL 3

GIANT SKULL

At up to 10 feet long, *Torosaurus'* skull is one of the longest ever found. The frill is more than half the length of the skull and has two large openings to make it lighter. Its skull and body are more lightly built than those of the massive *Triceratops*.

Length: Up to 25 ft.
Diet: Plants
Group: Ceratopsia
Family: Ceratopsidae

• *Torosaurus* is less common than *Triceratops*. Only one *Torosaurus* skull has been found for every 15 *Triceratops* skulls found.

Places to spot: Canada, USA
Habitat: Woodland and plains
When: 68–65 mya
Name means: Three-horned face
Alert: Sharp horns

TRICERATOPS
try-SER-a-tops

PLANT-EATER

LATE CRETACEOUS

DANGER LEVEL 4

Frill may
be used for
courtship display

USEFUL TIP!

This animal may
charge if scared!

LATECOMER

This famous dinosaur was
one of the last to appear
on Earth. It uses its huge,
sharp horns to defend
itself against predators,
including the mighty
Tyrannosaurus rex.

Horns are part
of skull

Sharp beak

Sometimes live
in herds but
usually solitary

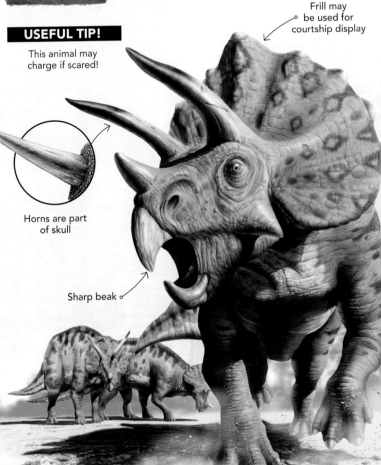

NO WAY!

With its powerful
jaws and batteries of
slicing cheek teeth,
Triceratops can chomp its
way through any type
of vegetation.

BIG HORN, LITTLE HORN

The two horns above its eyes can
grow to more than 3 feet long. The
horn on its nose is much smaller.

Length: Up to 30 ft.
Diet: Plants
Group: Ceratopsia
Family: Ceratopsidae

• Many *Triceratops* fossils have been found, suggesting it may be
the most common North American dinosaur in the Late Cretaceous.

TROODON

TROH-o-don

OMNIVORE

LATE CRETACEOUS

DANGER LEVEL 3

Place to spot: Canada, USA
Habitat: Woodland and plains
When: 99–75 mya
Name means: Wounding tooth
Alert: A long claw on each foot

CLEVER DINOSAUR

Troodon is a quick, clever dinosaur. Its eyes are forward-facing, giving it good eyesight and allowing it to judge distances accurately. It also has excellent hearing.

Feathers

Sharp, serrated teeth

Stiff tail held off the ground

NO WAY!

Troodon is one of the smartest dinosaurs, with a very large brain compared to its overall size.

Long front fingers

Sharp claw on second toe

MIXED DIET

The second toe of each of its back feet has a long, curved claw. Held off the ground while running, these claws are used to slash and kill prey. However, experts believe that *Troodon* also eats plants.

USEFUL TIP!

It's clever and cunning, making it hard to find.

Length: 10 ft.
Diet: Meat and plants
Group: Theropoda
Family: Troodontidae

• A number of *Troodon* nests have been discovered, some with fossilized baby *Troodons* still inside the eggs.

Places to spot: Canada, USA
Habitat: Open woodland
When: 67–65 mya
Name means: Tyrant lizard
Alert: Huge jaws

TYRANNOSAURUS
tie-RAN-oh-SAW-rus

MEAT-EATER

LATE CRETACEOUS

DANGER LEVEL 5

Nostril

Serrated teeth

PROTECTIVE BONES

Tyrannosaurus rex lives at the end of the Cretaceous, and preys on *Triceratops* and *Edmontosaurus*. It has a huge head and can gulp down 45 pounds of meat in one go.

NO WAY!

T. rex may hunt in packs, chasing prey over long distances to wear them out before pouncing and killing them.

MASSIVE JAWS

Tyrannosaurus has the largest, most powerful jaws of any predator.

Tail held out horizontally

Forward-pointing eyes

MIGHTY HUNTER

Tyrannosaurus has good eyesight, a good sense of smell, a strong jaw, and powerful legs. Its arms, however, are small and it has just two fingers. It survives through a combination of scavenging and actively hunting prey.

Clawed fingers

Sixty serrated teeth

USEFUL TIP!

May be covered in downy feathers.

This *Tyrannosaurus* has found a dead *Edmontosaurus* to feast on

Length: Up to 40 ft.
Diet: Meat
Group: Theropoda
Family: Tyrannosauridae

• *Tyrannosaurus* remains have been found that show clear signs of having been attacked by another *T. rex*—some survived, but others were partially eaten.

UBIRAJARA
YOU-bee-rah-JAH-rah

MEAT-EATER

EARLY CRETACEOUS

DANGER LEVEL 2

Place to spot: Brazil
Habitat: Coastal areas of an inland sea
When: 115 mya
Name means: Lord of the spear
Alert: May have had an elaborate dance

SHOULDER RIBBONS

It is difficult to miss *Ubirajara*'s unusual shoulder spikes, which are probably used for display. Only this dinosaur has such spikes, which are different from feathers, fur, or scales.

6-inch-long shoulder spikes

Bristles on the back and neck

Feathers

Very long tail

NO WAY!

Some scientists think *Ubirajara*'s shoulder spikes may have vibrated and possibly even made a noise!

USEFUL TIP!
May catch you by surprise when it leaps into the air to attract attention.

FEATHERED MANE

This dinosaur has a mane of bristles running along its back and neck. *Ubirajara* is the first feathered dinosaur to be found south of the equator.

Length: 5 ft.
Diet: Insects and small animals
Group: Theropoda
Family: Compsognathidae

• *Ubirajara*'s name means "lord of the spear" in the South American Tupi language, and it refers to the animal's shoulder spikes.

Place to spot: Brazil
Habitat: Forest
When: 225–200 mya
Name means: Black water lizard
Alert: No major weapons

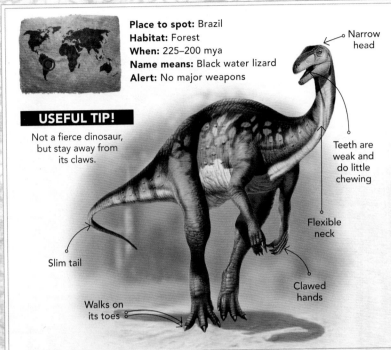

Narrow head

Teeth are weak and do little chewing

Flexible neck

Clawed hands

Slim tail

Walks on its toes

USEFUL TIP!

Not a fierce dinosaur, but stay away from its claws.

UNAYSAURUS
oo-NAH-ee-SAW-rus

PLANT-EATER

LATE TRIASSIC

DANGER LEVEL 1

SURVIVAL SKILL

This small, 165-pound prosauropod is one of the earliest known dinosaurs. *Unaysaurus* lives at a time when all the landmasses are connected to form the supercontinent Pangaea. It is closely related to *Plateosaurus*, the first giant sauropod.

Place to spot: USA
Habitat: Floodplains and scrub
When: 76 mya
Name means: Horned face from Utah
Alert: May charge using its nasal horn

USEFUL TIP!

Utahceratops can be found in herds with other herbivores.

Nose horn high on snout

Huge head

UTAHCERATOPS
YOO-tah-SER-a-tops

PLANT-EATER

LATE CRETACEOUS

DANGER LEVEL 3

NOSE HORN

Utahceratops' skull is huge. At about 8 feet long, it is longer than an average adult human is tall! If threatened by a predator, this dinosaur can inflict a lot of damage with the horn above its nostrils.

Length: 8 ft.
Diet: Plants
Group: Sauropodomorpha
Family: Prosauropoda

Length: 23 ft.
Diet: Plants
Group: Ceratopsia
Family: Ceratopsidae

UTAHRAPTOR

YOO-tah-RAP-tor

MEAT-EATER

EARLY CRETACEOUS

DANGER LEVEL 5

Place to spot: USA
Habitat: Open woodland
When: 126 mya
Name means: Thief from Utah
Alert: Lethal foot claw

USEFUL TIP!

This dinosaur has good eyesight. Don't let it see you!

Jaw lined with sharp teeth

GIANT KILLER

Utahraptor is a giant dromaeosaur, or birdlike theropod. It has a 9-inch sickle claw on each foot, which is its main weapon of attack. It weighs 1,100–1,500 pounds and is fast enough to catch anything smaller than itself.

LETHAL CLAWS

Utahraptor's claws may be used for stabbing or slashing its prey. Some scientists think that they can even be used for suffocating other animals to death.

Long tail for balance when running at speed

Long, grasping hand claws

NO WAY!

Like other dromaeosaurs, *Utahraptor* probably has long, colorful feathers on its arms and tail.

Large, sicklelike claw kept raised from the ground

STATELY DINOSAUR

Utahraptor is the state dinosaur of Utah.

Length: 20-23 ft.
Diet: Meat
Group: Theropoda
Family: Dromaeosauridae

• *Utahraptor* attacks by leaping on to the back of its prey, sickle claws first, and slashing downwards to rip its victim apart.

Places to spot: Mongolia, China
Habitat: Open woodland
When: 74–71 mya
Name means: Rapid thief
Alert: Fast-moving killer

VELOCIRAPTOR
ve-LOSS-i-RAP-tor

MEAT-EATER

LATE CRETACEOUS

DANGER LEVEL 5

Large eyes

SURVIVAL SKILL

Velociraptor is a lightly built, fast predator with a deadly, sickle-shaped claw on each foot. It has a relatively large brain and may have also been one of the most intelligent dinosaurs. It is also one of the most famous.

USEFUL TIP!

You'll need to be smart to escape this dinosaur!

Long, slender skull

Feathers insulate body

FEATHERS

Velociraptor is a feathered dinosaur. Knobs on its arms are the same as on a bird's wing bones where the feathers attach.

Stiff tail

Three long and narrow fingers with sharp claws

Claw on second toe

NO WAY!

In the Gobi Desert in 1971, a complete *Velociraptor* skeleton was found locked in a death grip with a *Protoceratops*.

LARGE BRAIN

This dinosaur has a large brain for its body size. Only troodontids may be bigger.

Length: Up to 6 ft.
Diet: Meat
Group: Theropoda
Family: Dromaeosauridae

• *Velociraptor* combines intelligence with a terrifying array of weapons, including hand claws and switchblade-knife foot claws.

WUERHOSAURUS

woo-uhr-huh-SAW-rus

PLANT-EATER

EARLY CRETACEOUS

DANGER LEVEL 3

Place to spot: China
Habitat: Tropical plains
When: 135–120 mya
Name means: Lizard from Wuerho
Alert: Dangerous tail

LAST OF THE STEGOSAURS

This armored Cretaceous dinosaur may be one of the last of the mighty stegosaurs, as most known stegosaurs are from the earlier Jurassic period.

NO WAY!

Wuerhosaurus' spiky defenses are vital because it is too slow and heavy to run.

Shapes of plates not known

16 bony plates along spine

Flexible, swinging tail ending in four sharp spikes

Forelimbs shorter than hind limbs

COMPARING PLATES

Like its American cousin *Stegosaurus*, *Wuerhosaurus* has four spikes on the end of its tail and a series of plates along its backbone. However, it is not known how they compared in shape to the tall, triangular ones of *Stegosaurus*.

USEFUL TIP!

Watch out for the sharp spikes on that swinging tail!

Length: Up to 26 ft.
Diet: Plants
Group: Stegosauria
Family: Stegosauridae

• *Wuerhosaurus'* head is lower to the ground than that of the Jurassic stegosaurids. It feeds on low-lying shrubs.

Place to spot: China
Habitat: Forest
When: 159–154 mya
Name means: Hidden dragon
Alert: Small and fast

YINLONG
yin-LONG

PLANT-EATER

LATE JURASSIC

DANGER LEVEL 1

Bony skull projections with short teeth

NO WAY!

Yinlong is the most primitive ceratopsian known to science. Its descendants include the mighty *Triceratops*.

Long, thin tail for balance when running

Horny beak

Five-fingered hands

BEAK BONE

The front of *Yinlong's* snout is equipped with a beak made of horn. It also has two fanglike teeth.

SURVIVAL SKILL

Yinlong is the only known Jurassic ceratopsian—all other ceratopsians are from the Cretaceous. It has bony projections on its skull that look like those of the pachycephalosaurs, or the "boneheads."

Three-toed foot

USEFUL TIP!

May feed in large herds.

Length: 10 ft.
Diet: Plants
Group: Cerapoda
Family: Ceratopsidae

• *Yinlong* is a small, two-legged plant-eater that is fast on its feet. It can dart away through foliage to escape predators.

INDEX